SCALES & MODES
MADE EASY

mobile
online
in print

Flame Tree Music
BOOKS • eBOOKS • RESOURCES

Publisher and Creative Director: Nick Wells
Project, design, notation and media integration: Jake Jackson
Website and software: David Neville with Stevens Dumpala and Steve Moulton
Editorial: Laura Bulbeck, Emma Chafer and Esme Chapman

Special thanks to: Jane Ashley, Frances Bodiam, Helen Crust,
Christine Delaborde, Stephen Feather, Sara Robson, Chris Herbert, Polly Prior,
Gail Sharkey, Mike Spender and Birgitta Williams.

Special thanks to Alan Brown for the scales notation

First published 2013 by
FLAME TREE PUBLISHING
Crabtree Hall, Crabtree Lane
Fulham, London SW6 6TY
United Kingdom
www.flametreepublishing.com

Music information site: www.flametreemusic.com

13 15 17 16 14
1 3 5 7 9 10 8 6 4 2

The CIP record for this book is available from the British Library.

Android is a trademark of Google Inc. Logic Pro, iPhone and iPad are either registered trademarks or trademarks of Apple Computer
Inc. in the United States and/or other countries. Cubase is a registered trademark or trademark of Steinberg Media Technologies
GmbH, a wholly owned subsidiary of Yamaha Corporation, in the United States and/or other countries. Nokia's product names are
either trademarks or registered trademarks of Nokia. Nokia is a registered trademark of Nokia Corporation in the United States and/or
other countries. Samsung and Galaxy S are both registered trademarks of Samsung Electronics America, Ltd. in the United States
and/or other countries.

Alan Brown (Engraving). A former member of the Scottish National Orchestra, Alan now works as a freelance musician, with several
leading UK orchestras, and as a consultant in music and IT. Alan has had several compositions published, developed a set of music
theory CD-Roms, co-written a series of Bass Guitar Examination Handbooks and worked on over 100 further titles.

Jake Jackson is a writer and musician. He has created and contributed to over 20 practical music books,
including *Songwriter's Rhyming Dictionary*, *Play Flamenco* and *Piano and Keyboard Chords*. His music is available
on iTunes, Amazon and Spotify amongst others.

ISBN: 978-0-85775-803-3

Printed in China

SCALES
& MODES
MADE EASY

SEE IT ▦ HEAR IT

COMPREHENSIVE SOUND LINKS

ALAN BROWN & JAKE JACKSON

**FLAME TREE
PUBLISHING**

A

A♯/B♭

B

C

C♯/D♭

D

D♯/E♭

E

F

F♯/G♭

G

G♯/A♭

Contents

FREE ACCESS on smartphones, iPhone, Android etc. Use any QR code app to scan this QR code

Or go straight to www.flametreemusic.com to **HEAR** chords, scales, and find more resources

Introducing the Scales

This useful new book will show you just about every scale you are likely to come across. For creative music making, either composition or improvisation, the more scales in more keys that you know the greater will be your flexibility and expressive capabilities. As an interpretative performer you will be able to understand better the music you are playing. We hope it will provide musicians of all levels with a solid point of reference that can be used to enhance music-making of all kinds.

The Anatomy of a Scale

Scales are invariably named after their starting note or tonic, also known as the key note, eg C in a C Major scale. It is common to number notes of a scale, with the tonic counting as one, so that we can refer to, for example, 'the fifth degree of the scale' or simply 'the fifth'. Depending on the range of your instrument, you are quite likely to be able to play higher or lower than the one-octave scales given in this book.

Abbreviation Used in Scale Patterns

For each of the scales and modes included in this book, we have included the scale pattern. This shows the relationship between each note in the scale. For example, the scale pattern of the **major scale** is:

T T S T T T S

S = semitone (USA half step); **T** = tone (whole step);

m3 = minor third (three semitones);

a2 = augmented second (also three semitones).

A

A♯/B♭

B

C

C♯/D♭

D

D♯/E♭

E

F

F♯/G♭

G

G♯/A♭

FREE ACCESS on smartphones, iPhone, Android etc. Use any QR code app to scan this QR code

Or go straight to www.flametreemusic.com to **HEAR** chords, scales, and find more resources

A

A#/B♭

B

C

C#/D♭

D

D#/E♭

E

F

F#/G♭

G

G#/A♭

Modes

Put simply, most scales can be recycled to generate more scales with different interval structures and therefore different sounds simply by starting the new scale on each degree of the old scale. The simplest example is the set of major scale modes, which appear in several groups.

- **Dorian**: contains the notes of the major scale starting from its second degree.
- **Phrygian**: contains the notes of the major scale starting from its third degree.
- **Lydian**: contains the notes of the major scale starting from its fourth degree.
- **Mixolydian**: contains the notes of the major scale starting from its fifth degree.
- **Aeolian**: contains the notes of the major scale starting from its sixth degree.
- **Locrian**: contains the notes of the major scale starting from its seventh degree.

Even though the major scale and its modal scales use the same notes, because they have different keynotes they do not have the same tonality. For example, while the major scale has a major third interval from the root to the third note and a major seventh interval from the root to the seventh note, in contrast, the Dorian modal scale has a flattened third interval from the root to the third note and a flattened seventh interval from the root to the seventh note, making it a type of minor scale.

Using Modes

Modal scales can be used for improvising and composing melodies. Two different approaches can be taken with regard to them:

- Advanced players sometimes use modal scales as chord scales (using a different mode over each chord).
- Modes can be treated as key centres in their own right, with a group of chords

FREE ACCESS on smartphones, iPhone, Android etc. Use any QR code app to scan this QR code

Or go straight to www.flametreemusic.com to **HEAR** chords, scales, and find more resources

6

to accompany each modal scale. For example, the D Dorian modal scale (see below) could be used over a D Dorian minor key centre containing any of the following chords: Dm, Em, F, G, Am, C.

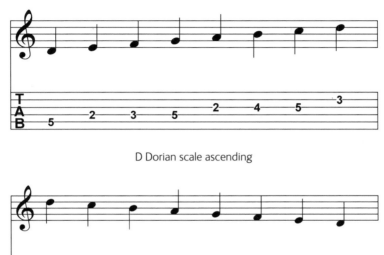

D Dorian scale ascending

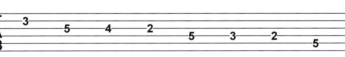

D Dorian scale descending

Scales and Modes

This book contains 18 of the most useful scales and modes, and there is one example of each for each of the 12 chromatic tones. We have divided the scales and modes included into four groups (**Major, Minor, Dominant** and **Unusual**), and for each have given a short description of how they are formed and in what style of music they might best be used.

Letters down the left margin: A, A#/B♭, B, C, C#/D♭, D, D#/E♭, E, F, F#/G♭, G, G#/A♭

THE MAJOR GROUP

The third degree is important in giving a scale its basic flavour and all scales in this group have a third (four semitones, e.g. C to E) and usually a major seventh (11 semitones, e.g. C to B). Some other scales with major thirds also have minor sevenths (10 semitones, e.g. C to Bb) and appear in the Dominant Group.

- **Major**: this is the most commonly used scale in western music, being the 'Doh, Re, Mi' scale used in *The Sound Of Music*.
  Scale Pattern: T T S T T T S

- **Major Pentatonic**: this is a major scale with gaps (no fourth or seventh) and can be heard in many traditional tunes from places as far apart as Scotland and China.
  Scale Pattern: T T m3 T m3

- The major scale gives rise to a set of modes, explained earlier in the book. One of these modes, the **Lydian**, is in this group. It resembles a major scale except for the raised fourth degree.
  Scale Pattern: T T T S T T S

- **Lydian Augmented**: this is a modal version of the melodic minor (starting on its parent scale's third step) and is essentially a lydian with a raised, or augmented, fifth. Like all scales with an altered fifth it is restless and used in modern jazz.
  Scale Pattern: T T T T S T S

THE MINOR GROUP

Here we are looking at a group of scales with minor thirds, which includes the scales commonly thought of as minor, several modal scales and a few unusual ones.

- **Natural Minor/Aeolian Mode**: this takes a major scale and starts on its sixth degree. Many folk and traditional tunes use this scale; significant notes are the flat six and seventh.
  Scale Pattern: T S T T S T T

- **Harmonic Minor**: this is identical to the natural minor except for the seventh degree, which is a semitone higher to make a major dominant chord possible, essential for most progressions in minor keys.
  Scale Pattern: T S T T S a2 S

- **Melodic Minor**: this is traditionally played with major sixth and seventh on the way up and lowered sixth and seventh on the way down. Improvising players often abandon the descending version and use exclusively the ascending form, which is consequently also called the Jazz Melodic Minor.
  Scale Pattern: T S T T T T S (ascending)

- **Dorian**: This is another important modal scale, also heard in jazz but in many folk songs too. Notice that it has a major sixth but a minor seventh.
  Scale Pattern: T S T T T S T

- **Minor Pentatonic**: is another variant, which could be thought of as a simplified minor scale with gaps. Like the major pentatonic, it

FREE ACCESS on smartphones, iPhone, Android etc. Use any QR code app to scan this QR code

Or go straight to www.flametreemusic.com to **HEAR** chords, scales, and find more resources

8

is often found in folk-melodies but also a favourite with rock guitarists.

Scale Pattern: m3 T T m3 T

• **Blues**: this is created by adding one chromatic note (a raised fourth or a flattened fifth) to the minor pentatonic scale. The blues scale can also be played over a dominant seventh chord.

Scale Pattern: m3 T S S m3 T

• **Phrygian**: this is another scale sometimes heard in jazz or folk music. It is identical to the aeolian/natural minor except for its lowered second step.

Scale Pattern: S T T T S T T

• **Locrian**: this takes the notes of the phrygian and lowers its fifth step which gives an unstable brooding quality to any music using it.

Scale Pattern: S T T S T T T

DOMINANT GROUP

The essential characteristics of dominant-type scales are the major third and minor (lowered) seventh.

• **Mixolydian**: this is the most obvious example of a dominant type scale, being simply a major scale starting on its fifth degree. You can also think of it as a major scale with a flattened seventh. Used in blues, rock, jazz and folk music.

Scale Pattern: T T S T T S T

• **Phrygian Major/Spanish Gypsy**: this scale starts on the fifth degree of the harmonic minor scale. Its features are the lowered second and seventh notes and it works well over a dominant chord with a flattened ninth. It is commonly used in flamenco and heavy metal music.

Scale Pattern: S a2 S T S T T

• **Lydian Dominant**: this is a mode of the melodic minor and has the sharp fourth of a lydian and the flat seventh of a mixolydian. Used mainly in jazz.

Scale Pattern: T T T S T S T

• **Diminished/Octatonic**: this is created by adding the two altered ninths from the previous scale to the lydian dominant. It has nine different notes and can only be transposed a couple of times before it starts to repeat the same notes. Used mainly in jazz.

Scale Pattern: S T S T S T S T

UNUSUAL SCALES

Most of these scales are used less than some of the earlier ones but may prove of interest in creating more experimental sounds.

• **Chromatic**: this can be used with any chord. As it contains **all twelve semitones** it can't be transposed or turned into a mode without stubbornly remaining itself.

• **Wholetone**: this also defies much transposition: if you took out every alternate note of the chromatic it would make one of the wholetone scales, the notes left making up the other. It will fit a dominant chord but with a little modification can give rise to a further set of modes.

Scale Pattern: T T T T T T

FREE ACCESS on smartphones, iPhone, Android etc. Use any QR code app to scan this QR code

Or go straight to www.flametreemusic.com to **HEAR** chords, scales, and find more resources

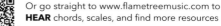

9

The Sound Links
A Quick Guide

Requirements: a camera and internet ready smartphone (eg. **iPhone**, any **Android** phone (e.g. **Samsung** Galaxy), **Nokia Lumia**, or **camera-enabled tablet** such as the **iPad** Mini). The best result is achieved using a WIFI connection.

1. Download any **free QR code reader**. An app store search will reveal a great many of these, so obviously it is best to go with the ones with the highest ratings and don't be afraid to try a few before you settle on the one that works best for you. Tapmedia's QR Reader app is good, or ATT Scanner (used below) or QR Media. Some of the free apps have ads, which can be annoying.

2. Find the scale you want to play, look at the diagram then check out the **QR code** at the base of the page.

FREE ACCESS on smartphones including iPhone & Android

Using any QR code app scan and **HEAR** the chord

76

3. On your smartphone, open the app and **scan** the **QR code** at the base of any particular scale page.

4. The QR reader app will take you to a browser, then the specific scale will be displayed on the flametreemusic.com website.

FREE ACCESS on smartphones, iPhone, Android etc. Use any QR code app to scan this QR code

Or go straight to www.flametreemusic.com to **HEAR** chords, scales, and find more resources

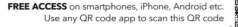

Sidebar note labels: A, A♯/B♭, B, C, C♯/D♭, D, D♯/E♭, E, F, F♯/G♭, G, G♯/A♭

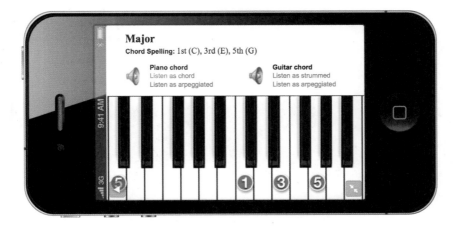

5. Using the usual pinch and zoom techniques, you can focus on the sound options.

6. Click the sounds! Both piano and guitar audio is provided. This is particularly helpful when you're playing with others.

Using the QR codes will give you direct access to all the scales on FlameTreeMusic.com. You can also access a wide range of chords.

FREE ACCESS on smartphones, iPhone, Android etc. Use any QR code app to scan this QR code

Or go straight to www.flametreemusic.com to **HEAR** chords, scales, and find more resources

SCALES & MODES

A

A

A♯/B♭

B

C

C♯/D♭

D

D♯/E♭

E

F

F♯/G♭

G

G♯/A♭

FREE ACCESS on smartphones, iPhone, Android etc.
Use any QR code app to scan this QR code

Or go straight to www.flametreemusic.com to
HEAR chords, scales, and find more resources

A Major

Scale pattern

A B C# D E F# G# A
A G# F# E D C# B A

Or go straight to www.flametreemusic.com to
HEAR chords, scales, and find more resources

A Major Pentatonic

Scale pattern	A B C♯ E F♯ A
	A F♯ E C♯ B A

A
A♯/B♭
B
C
C♯/D♭
D
D♯/E♭
E
F
F♯/G♭
G
G♯/A♭

FREE ACCESS on smartphones, iPhone, Android etc. Use any QR code app to scan this QR code

Or go straight to www.flametreemusic.com to **HEAR** chords, scales, and find more resources

15

A Lydian

A
A#/B♭
B
C
C#/D♭
D
D#/E♭
E
F
F#/G♭
G
G#/A♭

Scale pattern	A B C# D# E F# G# A
	A G# F# E D# C# B A

FREE ACCESS on smartphones, iPhone, Android etc.
Use any QR code app to scan this QR code

Or go straight to www.flametreemusic.com to
HEAR chords, scales, and find more resources

16

A Lydian Augmented

Scale pattern	A B C# D# E# F# G# A
	A G# F# E# D# C# B A

FREE ACCESS on smartphones, iPhone, Android etc.
Use any QR code app to scan this QR code

Or go straight to www.flametreemusic.com to
HEAR chords, scales, and find more resources

A
A#/B♭
B
C
C#/D♭
D
D#/E♭
E
F
F#/G♭
G
G#/A♭

A Natural Minor

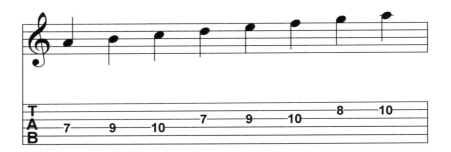

Scale pattern	A B C D E F G A
	A G F E D C B A

Or go straight to www.flametreemusic.com to
HEAR chords, scales, and find more resources

A Harmonic Minor

| Scale pattern | A B C D E F G# A
A G# F E D C B A |

A

A#/B♭

B

C

C#/D♭

D

D#/E♭

E

F

F#/G♭

G

G#/A♭

A

A Melodic Minor

Scale pattern

A B C D E F♯ G♯ A
A G♮ F♮ E D C B A

FREE ACCESS on smartphones, iPhone, Android etc.
Use any QR code app to scan this QR code

Or go straight to www.flametreemusic.com to
HEAR chords, scales, and find more resources

A Dorian

Scale pattern	A B C D E F#G A
	A G F#E D C B A

FREE ACCESS on smartphones, iPhone, Android etc. Use any QR code app to scan this QR code

Or go straight to www.flametreemusic.com to **HEAR** chords, scales, and find more resources

A

A#/B♭

B

C

C#/D♭

D

D#/E♭

E

F

F#/G♭

G

G#/A♭

A Minor Pentatonic

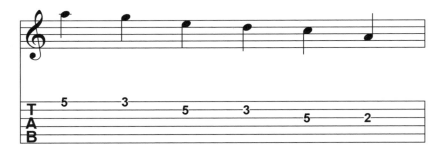

Scale pattern	A C D E G A
	A G E D C A

FREE ACCESS on smartphones, iPhone, Android etc. Use any QR code app to scan this QR code

Or go straight to www.flametreemusic.com to **HEAR** chords, scales, and find more resources

A Blues

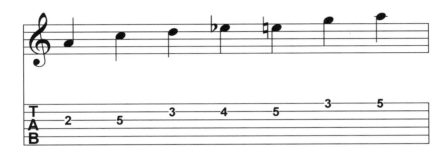

| Scale pattern | A C D E♭ E♮ G A
A G E♮ E♭ D C A |

Or go straight to www.flametreemusic.com to
HEAR chords, scales, and find more resources

A
A#/B♭
B
C
C#/D♭
D
D#/E♭
E
F
F#/G♭
G
G#/A♭

A Phrygian

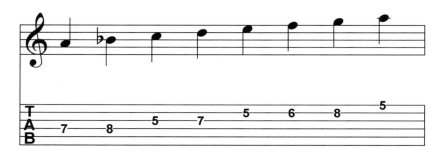

Scale pattern	A B♭ C D E F G A
	A G F E D C B♭ A

Or go straight to www.flametreemusic.com to
HEAR chords, scales, and find more resources

A Locrian

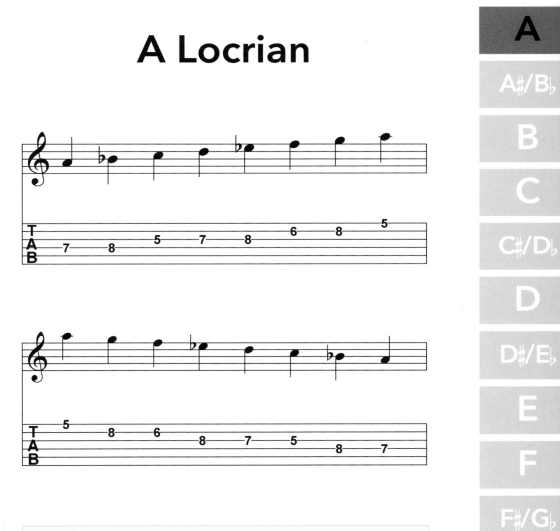

| Scale pattern | A B♭ C D E♭ F G A |
| | A G F E♭ D C B♭ A |

Or go straight to www.flametreemusic.com to
HEAR chords, scales, and find more resources

A Mixolydian

Scale pattern

A B C♯ D E F♯ G A
A G F♯ E D C♯ B A

Or go straight to www.flametreemusic.com to
HEAR chords, scales, and find more resources

A Phrygian Major
(Spanish Gypsy)

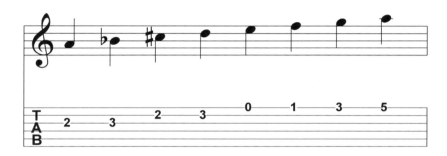

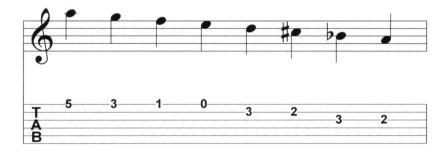

Scale pattern	A B♭ C♯ D E F G A
	A G F E D C♯ B♭ A

Or go straight to www.flametreemusic.com to **HEAR** chords, scales, and find more resources

A Lydian Dominant

Scale pattern	A B C♯ D♯ E F♯ G A
	A G F♯ E D♯ C♯ B A

A Diminished

Scale pattern	A B♭ C D♭ E♭ E♮ F♯ G A
	A G F♯ E E♭ D♭ C B♭ A

FREE ACCESS on smartphones, iPhone, Android etc.
Use any QR code app to scan this QR code

Or go straight to www.flametreemusic.com to
HEAR chords, scales, and find more resources

A
A♯/B♭
B
C
C♯/D♭
D
D♯/E♭
E
F
F♯/G♭
G
G♯/A♭

A Chromatic

A

A#/Bb

B

C

C#/Db

D

D#/Eb

E

F

F#/Gb

G

G#/Ab

Scale pattern

A Bb B♮ C C# D D# E F F# G G# A
A G# G♮ F# F♮ E D# D♮ C# C♮ B Bb A

FREE ACCESS on smartphones, iPhone, Android etc.
Use any QR code app to scan this QR code

Or go straight to www.flametreemusic.com to
HEAR chords, scales, and find more resources

A Wholetone

| Scale pattern | A B C# D# F G A |
| | A G F D# C# B A |

A
A#/Bb
B
C
C#/Db
D
D#/Eb
E
F
F#/Gb
G
G#/Ab

FREE ACCESS on smartphones, iPhone, Android etc.
Use any QR code app to scan this QR code

Or go straight to www.flametreemusic.com to
HEAR chords, scales, and find more resources

31

SCALES & MODES

A#B♭

A

A#/B♭

B

C

C#/D♭

D

D#/E♭

E

F

F#/G♭

G

G#/A♭

FREE ACCESS on smartphones, iPhone, Android etc.
Use any QR code app to scan this QR code

Or go straight to www.flametreemusic.com to
HEAR chords, scales, and find more resources

B♭ Major

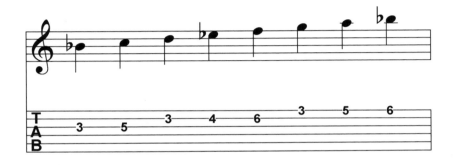

Scale pattern	B♭ C D E♭ F G A B♭
	B♭ A G F E♭ D C B♭

Or go straight to www.flametreemusic.com to
HEAR chords, scales, and find more resources

Sidebar navigation:
A
A#/B♭
B
C
C#/D♭
D
D#/E♭
E
F
F#/G♭
G
G#/A♭

Bb Major Pentatonic

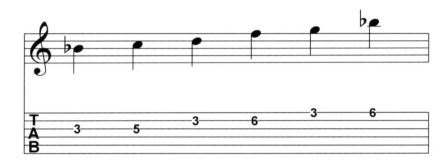

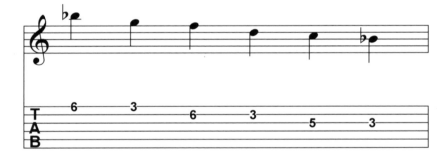

Scale pattern	Bb C D F G Bb
	Bb G F D C Bb

A

A#/Bb

B

C

C#/Db

D

D#/Eb

E

F

F#/Gb

G

G#/Ab

B♭ Lydian

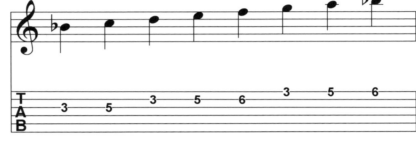

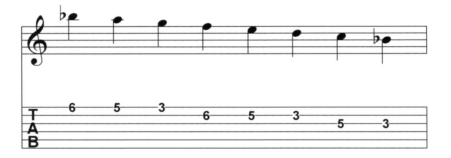

Scale pattern	B♭ C D E F G A B♭
	B♭ A G F E D C B♭

Or go straight to www.flametreemusic.com to
HEAR chords, scales, and find more resources

B♭ Lydian Augmented

Scale pattern	B♭ C D E F♯ G A B♭
	B♭ A G F♯ E D C B♭

Or go straight to www.flametreemusic.com to **HEAR** chords, scales, and find more resources

B♭ Natural Minor

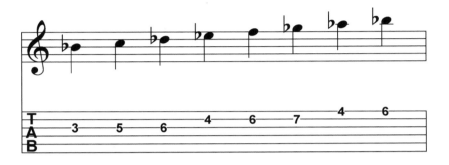

Scale pattern	B♭ C D♭ E♭ F G♭ A♭ B♭
	B♭ A♭ G♭ F E♭ D♭ C B♭

FREE ACCESS on smartphones, iPhone, Android etc. Use any QR code app to scan this QR code

Or go straight to www.flametreemusic.com to **HEAR** chords, scales, and find more resources

A
A#/B♭
B
C
C#/D♭
D
D#/E♭
E
F
F#/G♭
G
G#/A♭

B♭ Harmonic Minor

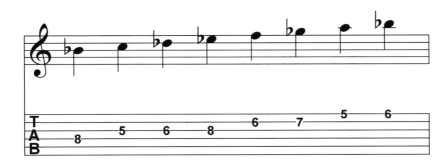

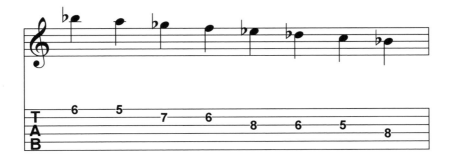

Scale pattern	B♭ C D♭ E♭ F G♭ A B♭
	B♭ A G♭ F E♭ D♭ C B♭

FREE ACCESS on smartphones, iPhone, Android etc. Use any QR code app to scan this QR code

Or go straight to www.flametreemusic.com to **HEAR** chords, scales, and find more resources

B♭ Melodic Minor

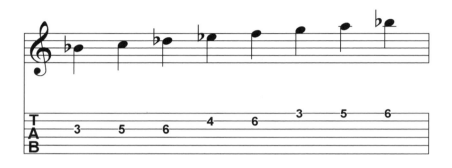

Scale pattern	B♭ C D♭ E♭ F G A B♭
	B♭ A♭ G♭ F E♭ D♭ C B♭

FREE ACCESS on smartphones, iPhone, Android etc. Use any QR code app to scan this QR code

Or go straight to www.flametreemusic.com to **HEAR** chords, scales, and find more resources

B♭ Dorian

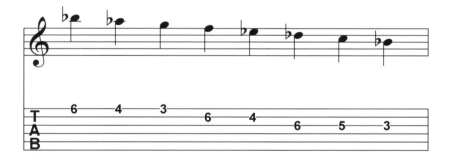

Scale pattern	B♭ C D♭ E♭ F G A♭ B♭
	B♭ A♭ G F E♭ D♭ C B♭

B♭ Minor Pentatonic

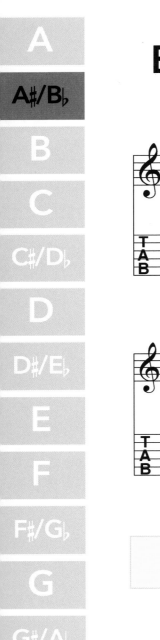

Scale pattern	B♭ D♭ E♭ F A♭ B♭
	B♭ A♭ F E♭ D♭ B♭

FREE ACCESS on smartphones, iPhone, Android etc.
Use any QR code app to scan this QR code

Or go straight to www.flametreemusic.com to
HEAR chords, scales, and find more resources

B♭ Blues

Scale pattern	B♭ D♭ E♭ F♭ F♮ A♭ B♭
	B♭ A♭ F♮ F♭ E♭ D♭ B♭

FREE ACCESS on smartphones, iPhone, Android etc. Use any QR code app to scan this QR code

Or go straight to www.flametreemusic.com to **HEAR** chords, scales, and find more resources

43

A♯ Phrygian

Scale pattern	A♯ B C♯ D♯ E♯ F♯ G♯ A♯
	A♯ G♯ F♯ E♯ D♯ C♯ B A♯

FREE ACCESS on smartphones, iPhone, Android etc. Use any QR code app to scan this QR code

Or go straight to www.flametreemusic.com to **HEAR** chords, scales, and find more resources

44

A♯ Locrian

Scale pattern	A♯ B C♯ D♯ E F♯ G♯ A♯
	A♯ G♯ F♯ E D♯ C♯ B A♯

A
A♯/B♭
B
C
C♯/D♭
D
D♯/E♭
E
F
F♯/G♭
G
G♯/A♭

B♭ Mixolydian

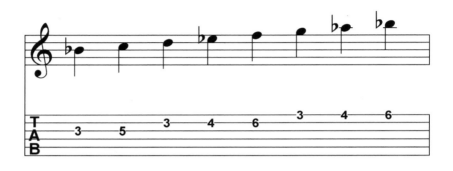

| **Scale pattern** | B♭ C D E♭ F G A♭ B♭ |
| | B♭ A♭ G F E♭ D C B♭ |

B♭ Phrygian Major
(Spanish Gypsy)

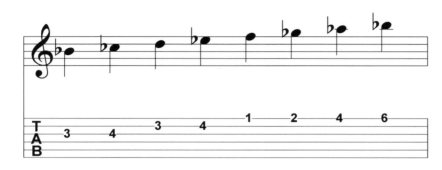

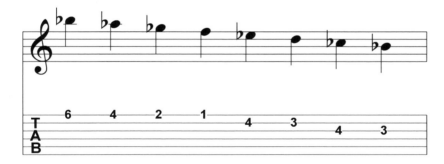

Scale pattern	B♭ C♭ D E♭ F G♭ A♭ B♭
	B♭ A♭ G♭ F E♭ D C♭ B♭

B♭ Lydian Dominant

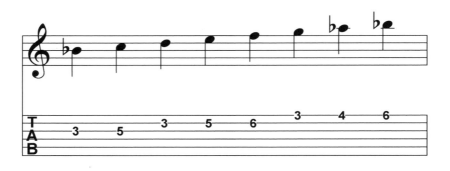

Scale pattern	B♭ C D E F G A♭ B♭
	B♭ A♭ G F E D C B♭

B♭ Diminished

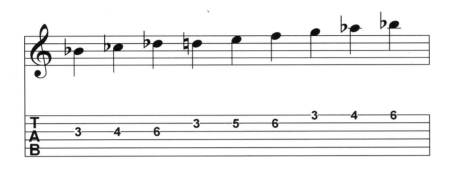

Scale pattern	B♭ C♭ D♭ D♮ E F G A♭ B♭
	B♭ A♭ G F E D♮ D♭ C♭ B♭

Or go straight to www.flametreemusic.com to **HEAR** chords, scales, and find more resources

Sidebar navigation:
A
A♯/B♭
B
C
C♯/D♭
D
D♯/E♭
E
F
F♯/G♭
G
G♯/A♭

B♭ Chromatic

Scale pattern

B♭ C♭ C♮ D♭ D♮ E♭ E♮ F G♭ G♮ A♭ A♮ B♭
B♭ A A♭ G G♭ F E E♭ D D♭ C C♭ B♭

Or go straight to www.flametreemusic.com to
HEAR chords, scales, and find more resources

B♭ Wholetone

Scale pattern	B♭ C D E G♭ A♭ B♭
	B♭ A♭ G♭ E D C B♭

SCALES & MODES

B

A
A#/B♭
B
C
C#/D♭
D
D#/E♭
E
F
F#/G♭
G
G#/A♭

B Major

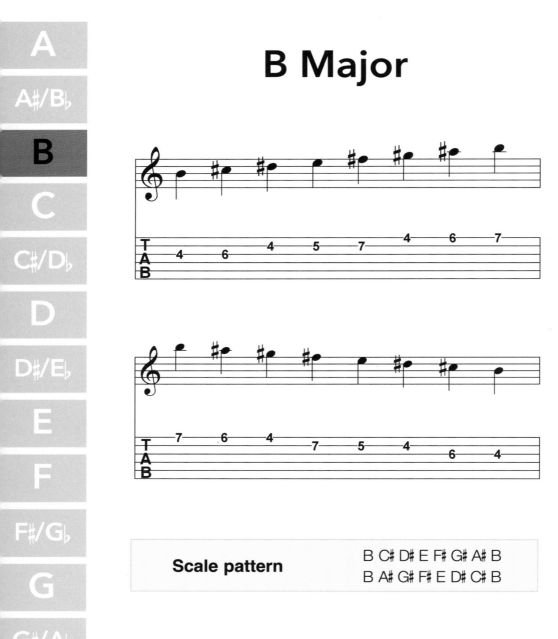

Scale pattern	B C# D# E F# G# A# B
	B A# G# F# E D# C# B

FREE ACCESS on smartphones, iPhone, Android etc.
Use any QR code app to scan this QR code

Or go straight to www.flametreemusic.com to
HEAR chords, scales, and find more resources

54

B Major Pentatonic

Scale pattern	B C# D# F# G# B
	B G# F# D# C# B

B Lydian

Scale pattern	B C# D# E# F# G# A# B
	B A# G# F# E# D# C# B

B Lydian Augmented

Scale pattern	B C# D# E# Fx G# A# B
	B A# G# Fx E# D# C# B

FREE ACCESS on smartphones, iPhone, Android etc.
Use any QR code app to scan this QR code

Or go straight to www.flametreemusic.com to
HEAR chords, scales, and find more resources

B Natural Minor

Scale pattern	B C# D E F# G A B
	B A G F# E D C# B

FREE ACCESS on smartphones, iPhone, Android etc. Use any QR code app to scan this QR code

Or go straight to www.flametreemusic.com to **HEAR** chords, scales, and find more resources

B Harmonic Minor

| Scale pattern | B C♯ D E F♯ G A♯ B |
| | B A♯ G F♯ E D C♯ B |

B Melodic Minor

Scale pattern	B C♯ D E F♯ G♯ A♯ B
	B A♮ G♮ F♯ E D C♯ B

FREE ACCESS on smartphones, iPhone, Android etc.
Use any QR code app to scan this QR code

Or go straight to www.flametreemusic.com to
HEAR chords, scales, and find more resources

B Dorian

Scale pattern	B C# D E F# G# A B
	B A G# F# E D C# B

A

A♯/B♭

B

C

C♯/D♭

D

D♯/E♭

E

F

F♯/G♭

G

G♯/A♭

B Minor Pentatonic

| Scale pattern | B D E F# A B |
| | B A F# E D B |

FREE ACCESS on smartphones, iPhone, Android etc.
Use any QR code app to scan this QR code

Or go straight to www.flametreemusic.com to
HEAR chords, scales, and find more resources

B Blues

A
A♯/B♭
B
C
C♯/D♭
D
D♯/E♭
E
F
F♯/G♭
G
G♯/A♭

Scale pattern

B D E F♮ F♯ A B
B A F♯ F♮ E D B

Or go straight to www.flametreemusic.com to
HEAR chords, scales, and find more resources

B Phrygian

A
A#/Bb
B
C
C#/Db
D
D#/Eb
E
F
F#/Gb
G
G#/Ab

Scale pattern

B C D E F# G A B
B A G F# E D C B

FREE ACCESS on smartphones, iPhone, Android etc. Use any QR code app to scan this QR code

Or go straight to www.flametreemusic.com to **HEAR** chords, scales, and find more resources

B Locrian

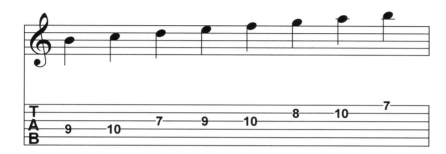

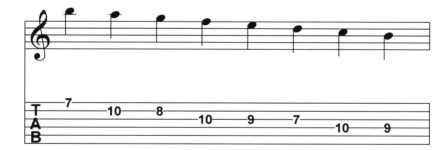

Scale pattern	B C D E F G A B B A G F E D C B

Or go straight to www.flametreemusic.com to
HEAR chords, scales, and find more resources

A
A♯/B♭
B
C
C♯/D♭
D
D♯/E♭
E
F
F♯/G♭
G
G♯/A♭

B Mixolydian

Scale pattern	B C# D# E F# G# A B
	B A G# F# E D# C# B

Or go straight to www.flametreemusic.com to **HEAR** chords, scales, and find more resources

B Phrygian Major
(Spanish Gypsy)

Scale pattern	B C D♯ E F♯ G A B
	B A G F♯ E D♯ C B

Or go straight to www.flametreemusic.com to
HEAR chords, scales, and find more resources

A

A♯/B♭

B

C

C♯/D♭

D

D♯/E♭

E

F

F♯/G♭

G

G♯/A♭

B Lydian Dominant

Scale pattern	B C# D# E# F# G# A B
	B A G# F# E# D# C# B

B Diminished

A
A#/B♭
B
C
C#/D♭
D
D#/E♭
E
F
F#/G♭
G
G#/A♭

| Scale pattern | B C D E♭ F F# G# A B |
| | B A G# F# F♮ E♭ D C B |

FREE ACCESS on smartphones, iPhone, Android etc.
Use any QR code app to scan this QR code

Or go straight to www.flametreemusic.com to
HEAR chords, scales, and find more resources

B Chromatic

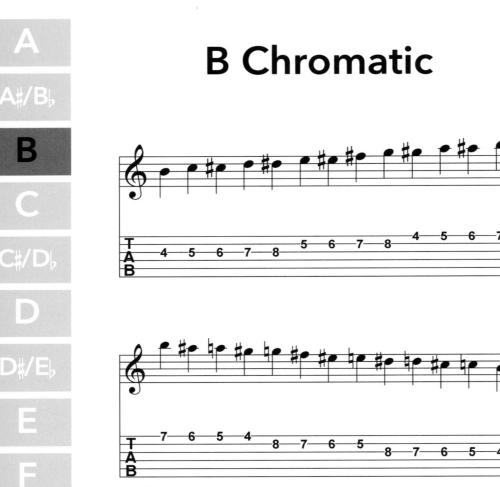

Scale pattern	B C C♯ D D♯ E E♯ F♯ G G♯ A A♯ B
	B A♯ A♮ G♯ G♮ F♯ E♯ E♮ D♯ D♮ C♯ C♮ B

Or go straight to www.flametreemusic.com to **HEAR** chords, scales, and find more resources

A
A♯/B♭
B
C
C♯/D♭
D
D♯/E♭
E
F
F♯/G♭
G
G♯/A♭

B Wholetone

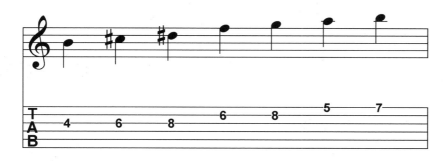

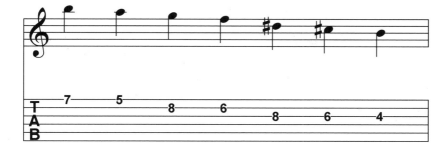

Scale pattern	B C# D# F G A B
	B A G F D# C# B

FREE ACCESS on smartphones, iPhone, Android etc.
Use any QR code app to scan this QR code

Or go straight to www.flametreemusic.com to
HEAR chords, scales, and find more resources

A

A#/Bb

B

C

C#/Db

D

D#/Eb

E

F

F#/Gb

G

G#/Ab

SCALES & MODES

C

A

A♯/B♭

B

C

C♯/D♭

D

D♯/E♭

E

F

F♯/G♭

G

G♯/A♭

FREE ACCESS on smartphones, iPhone, Android etc.
Use any QR code app to scan this QR code

Or go straight to www.flametreemusic.com to
HEAR chords, scales, and find more resources

C Major

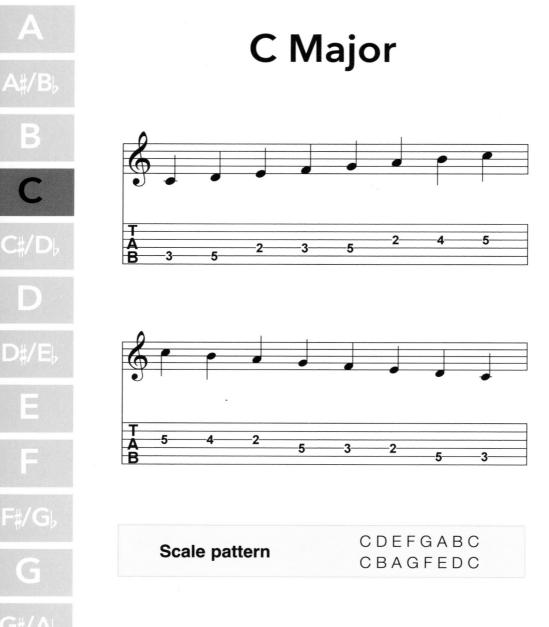

Scale pattern	C D E F G A B C
	C B A G F E D C

FREE ACCESS on smartphones, iPhone, Android etc.
Use any QR code app to scan this QR code

Or go straight to www.flametreemusic.com to
HEAR chords, scales, and find more resources

C Major Pentatonic

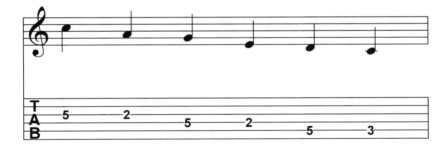

Scale pattern	C D E F G A B C C B A G F E D C

A

A#/B♭

B

C

C#/D♭

D

D#/E♭

E

F

F#/G♭

G

G#/A♭

Or go straight to www.flametreemusic.com to
HEAR chords, scales, and find more resources

C Lydian

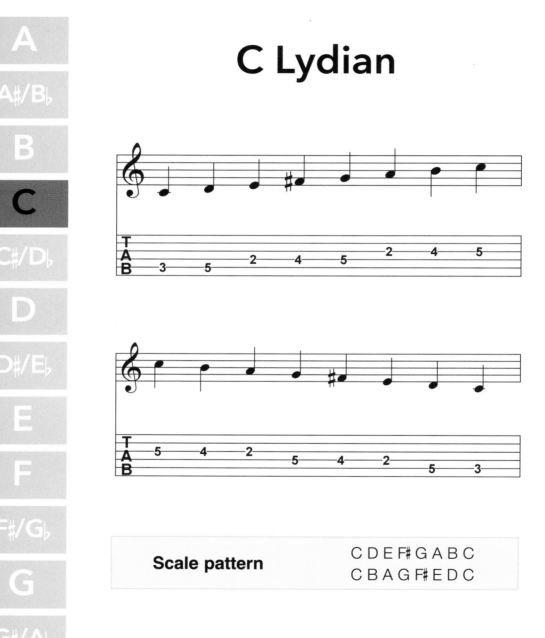

Scale pattern	C D E F♯ G A B C
	C B A G F♯ E D C

FREE ACCESS on smartphones, iPhone, Android etc.
Use any QR code app to scan this QR code

Or go straight to www.flametreemusic.com to
HEAR chords, scales, and find more resources

C Lydian Augmented

| **Scale pattern** | C D E F# G# A B C |
| | C B A G# F# E D C |

A
A#/Bb
B
C
C#/Db
D
D#/Eb
E
F
F#/Gb
G
G#/Ab

C Natural Minor

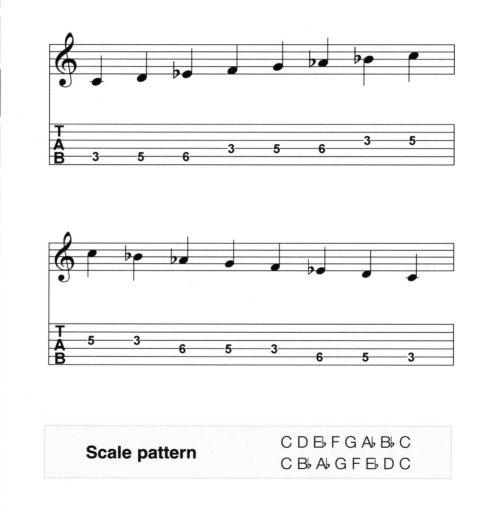

Scale pattern	C D E♭ F G A♭ B♭ C
	C B♭ A♭ G F E♭ D C

Or go straight to www.flametreemusic.com to **HEAR** chords, scales, and find more resources

Left sidebar navigation:
A
A#/B♭
B
C
C#/D♭
D
D#/E♭
E
F
F#/G♭
G
G#/A♭

C Harmonic Minor

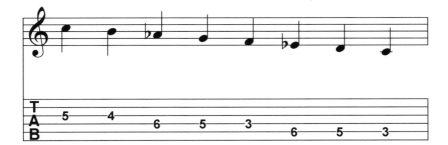

Scale pattern	C D E♭ F G A♭ B C
	C B A♭ G F E♭ D C

C Melodic Minor

| Scale pattern | C D E♭ F G A B C |
| | C B♭ A♭ G F E♭ D C |

FREE ACCESS on smartphones, iPhone, Android etc.
Use any QR code app to scan this QR code

Or go straight to www.flametreemusic.com to
HEAR chords, scales, and find more resources

C Dorian

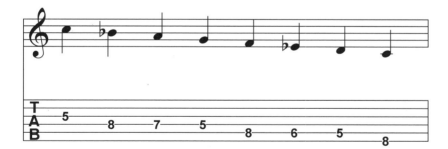

Scale pattern	C D E♭ F G A B♭ C
	C B♭ A G F E♭ D C

A
A♯/B♭
B
C
C♯/D♭
D
D♯/E♭
E
F
F♯/G♭
G
G♯/A♭

FREE ACCESS on smartphones, iPhone, Android etc.
Use any QR code app to scan this QR code

Or go straight to www.flametreemusic.com to
HEAR chords, scales, and find more resources

81

C Minor Pentatonic

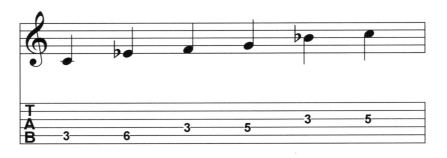

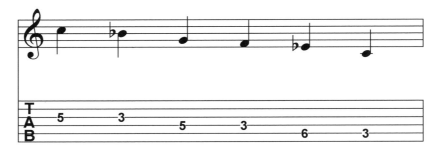

Scale pattern	C E♭ F G B♭ C
	C B♭ G F E♭ C

C Blues

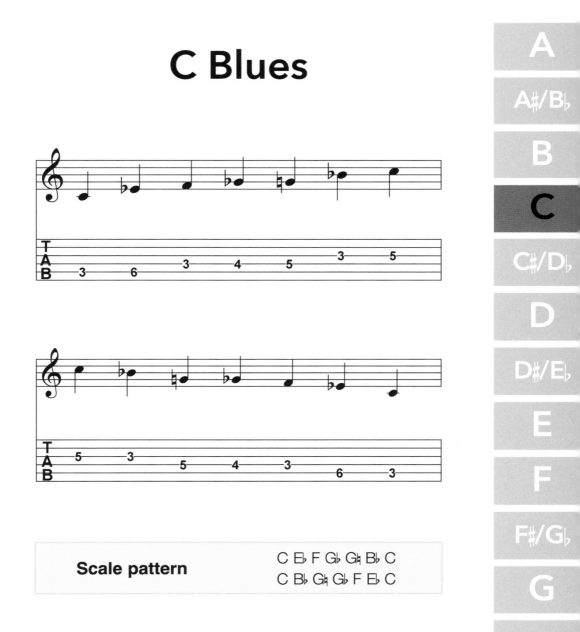

Scale pattern

C E♭ F G♭ G♮ B♭ C
C B♭ G♮ G♭ F E♭ C

Or go straight to www.flametreemusic.com to
HEAR chords, scales, and find more resources

C Phrygian

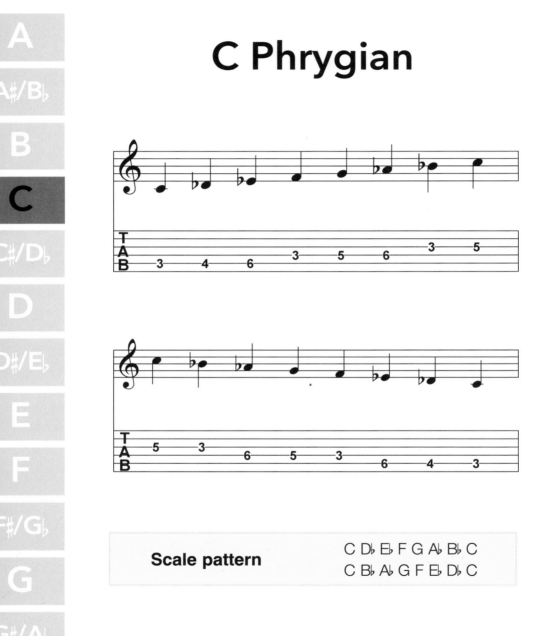

Scale pattern	C D♭ E♭ F G A♭ B♭ C
	C B♭ A♭ G F E♭ D♭ C

Or go straight to www.flametreemusic.com to
HEAR chords, scales, and find more resources

C Locrian

Scale pattern	C D♭ E♭ F G♭ A♭ B♭ C
	C B♭ A♭ G♭ F E♭ D♭ C

A
A♯/B♭
B
C
C♯/D♭
D
D♯/E♭
E
F
F♯/G♭
G
G♯/A♭

C Mixolydian

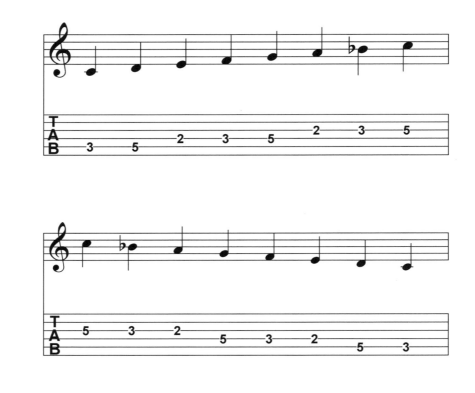

Scale pattern	C D E F G A B♭ C C B♭ A G F E D C

C Phrygian Major
(Spanish Gypsy)

Scale pattern	C D♭ E F G A♭ B♭ C
	C B♭ A♭ G F E D♭ C

A

A♯/B♭

B

C

C♯/D♭

D

D♯/E♭

E

F

F♯/G♭

G

G♯/A♭

Or go straight to www.flametreemusic.com to **HEAR** chords, scales, and find more resources

C Lydian Dominant

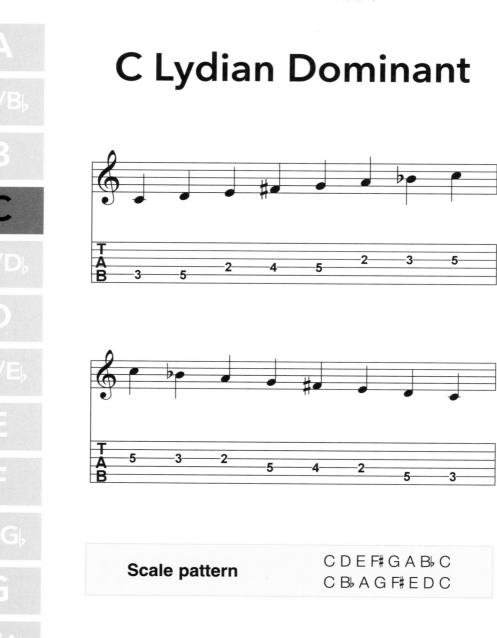

Scale pattern

C D E F♯ G A B♭ C
C B♭ A G F♯ E D C

FREE ACCESS on smartphones, iPhone, Android etc.
Use any QR code app to scan this QR code

Or go straight to www.flametreemusic.com to
HEAR chords, scales, and find more resources

C Diminished

Scale pattern	C D♭ E♭ E♮ F♯ G A B♭ C
	C B♭ A G F♯ E♮ E♭ D♭ C

A
A♯/B♭
B
C
C♯/D♭
D
D♯/E♭
E
F
F♯/G♭
G
G♯/A♭

C Chromatic

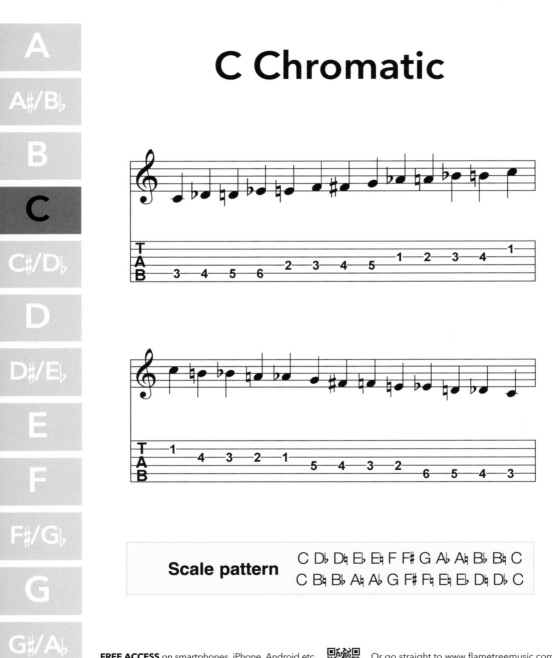

Scale pattern C Db Db Eb Eb F F# G Ab Ab Bb Bb C
C Bb Bb Ab Ab G F# Fb Eb Eb Db Db C

C Wholetone

A

A#/B♭

B

C

C#/D♭

D

D#/E♭

E

F

F#/G♭

G

G#/A♭

| Scale pattern | C D E F# G# A# C |
| | C A# G# F# E D C |

SCALES
& MODES

C# D♭

A

A#/B♭

B

C

C#/D♭

D

D#/E♭

E

F

F#/G♭

G

G#/A♭

FREE ACCESS on smartphones, iPhone, Android etc.
Use any QR code app to scan this QR code

Or go straight to www.flametreemusic.com to
HEAR chords, scales, and find more resources

D♭ Major

| Scale pattern | D♭ E♭ F G♭ A♭ B♭ C D♭ |
| | D♭ C B♭ A♭ G♭ F E♭ D♭ |

A
A#/B♭
B
C
C#/D♭
D
D#/E♭
E
F
F#/G♭
G
G#/A♭

D♭ Major Pentatonic

Scale pattern

D♭ E♭ F A♭ B♭ D♭
D♭ B♭ A♭ F E♭ D♭

D♭ Lydian

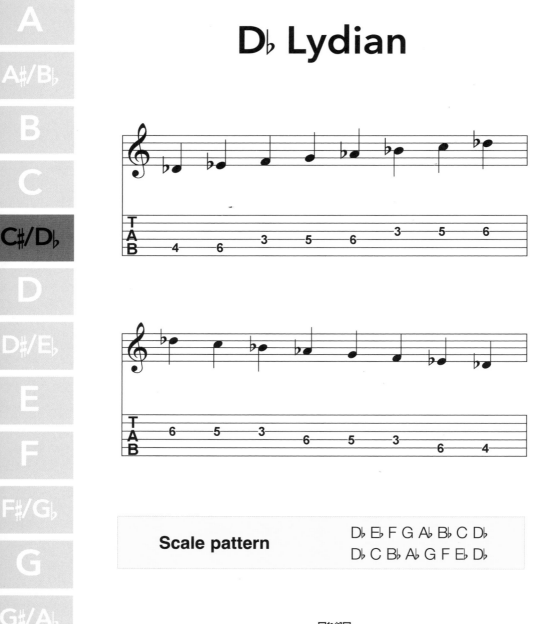

Scale pattern

D♭ E♭ F G A♭ B♭ C D♭
D♭ C B♭ A♭ G F E♭ D♭

D♭ Lydian Augmented

A

A♯/B♭

B

C

C♯/D♭

D

D♯/E♭

E

F

F♯/G♭

G

G♯/A♭

Scale pattern	D♭ E♭ F G A B♭ C D♭
	D♭ C B♭ A G F E♭ D♭

FREE ACCESS on smartphones, iPhone, Android etc.
Use any QR code app to scan this QR code

Or go straight to www.flametreemusic.com to
HEAR chords, scales, and find more resources

C♯ Natural Minor

Scale pattern	C♯ D♯ E F♯ G♯ A B C♯
	C♯ B A G♯ F♯ E D♯ C♯

FREE ACCESS on smartphones, iPhone, Android etc. Use any QR code app to scan this QR code

Or go straight to www.flametreemusic.com to **HEAR** chords, scales, and find more resources

C♯ Harmonic Minor

A

A♯/B♭

B

C

C♯/D♭

D

D♯/E♭

E

F

F♯/G♭

G

G♯/A♭

Scale pattern	C♯ D♯ E F♯ G♯ A B♯ C♯
	C♯ B♯ A G♯ F♯ E D♯ C♯

FREE ACCESS on smartphones, iPhone, Android etc. Use any QR code app to scan this QR code

Or go straight to www.flametreemusic.com to **HEAR** chords, scales, and find more resources

C♯ Melodic Minor

Scale pattern

C♯ D♯ E F♯ G♯ A♯ B♯ C♯
C♯ B♮ A♮ G♯ F♯ E D♯ C♯

C♯ Dorian

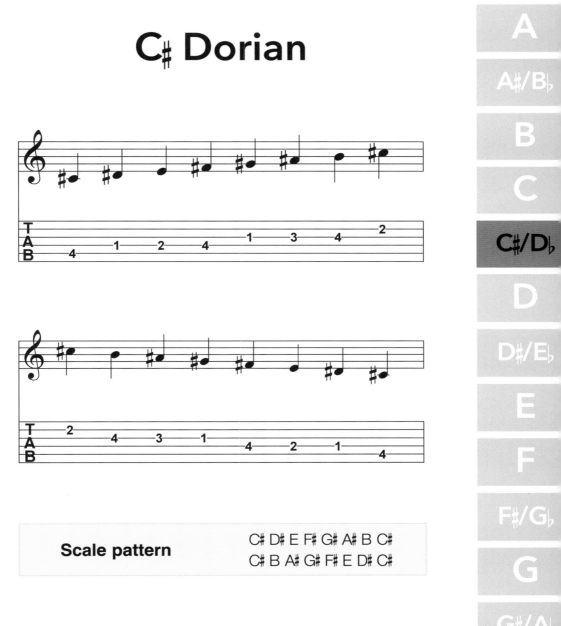

Scale pattern	C♯ D♯ E F♯ G♯ A♯ B C♯
	C♯ B A♯ G♯ F♯ E D♯ C♯

FREE ACCESS on smartphones, iPhone, Android etc. Use any QR code app to scan this QR code

Or go straight to www.flametreemusic.com to **HEAR** chords, scales, and find more resources

C♯ Minor Pentatonic

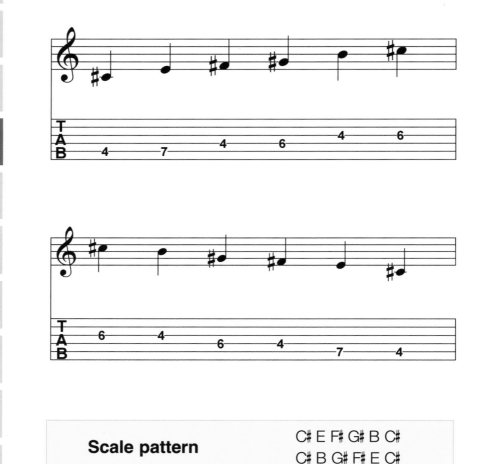

Scale pattern	C♯ E F♯ G♯ B C♯
	C♯ B G♯ F♯ E C♯

Or go straight to www.flametreemusic.com to **HEAR** chords, scales, and find more resources

C♯ Blues

| Scale pattern | C♯ E F♯ G♮ G♯ B C♯ |
| | C♯ B G♯ G♮ F♯ E C♯ |

Or go straight to www.flametreemusic.com to
HEAR chords, scales, and find more resources

A

A♯/B♭

B

C

C♯/D♭

D

D♯/E♭

E

F

F♯/G♭

G

G♯/A♭

C♯ Phrygian

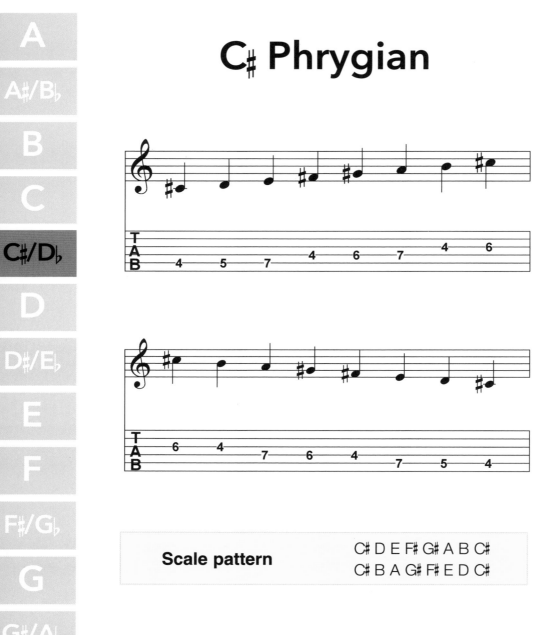

Scale pattern	C♯ D E F♯ G♯ A B C♯
	C♯ B A G♯ F♯ E D C♯

FREE ACCESS on smartphones, iPhone, Android etc. Use any QR code app to scan this QR code

Or go straight to www.flametreemusic.com to **HEAR** chords, scales, and find more resources

C♯ Locrian

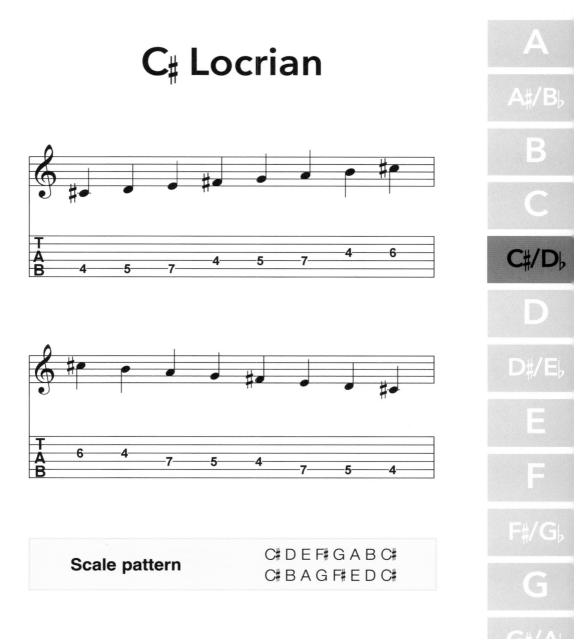

Scale pattern	C♯ D E F♯ G A B C♯
	C♯ B A G F♯ E D C♯

FREE ACCESS on smartphones, iPhone, Android etc. Use any QR code app to scan this QR code

Or go straight to www.flametreemusic.com to **HEAR** chords, scales, and find more resources

C# Mixolydian

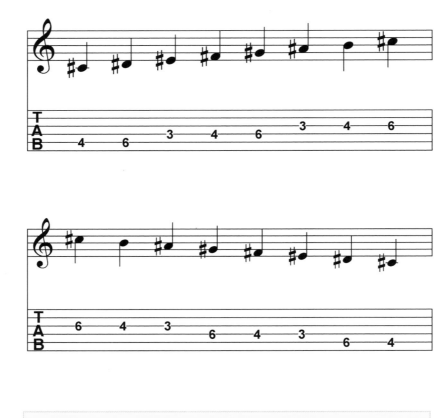

Scale pattern	C# D# E# F# G# A# B C#
	C# B A# G# F# E# D# C#

FREE ACCESS on smartphones, iPhone, Android etc. Use any QR code app to scan this QR code

Or go straight to www.flametreemusic.com to **HEAR** chords, scales, and find more resources

C# Phrygian Major
(Spanish Gypsy)

Scale pattern	C# D E# F# G# A B C#
	C# B A G# F# E# D C#

D♭ Lydian Dominant

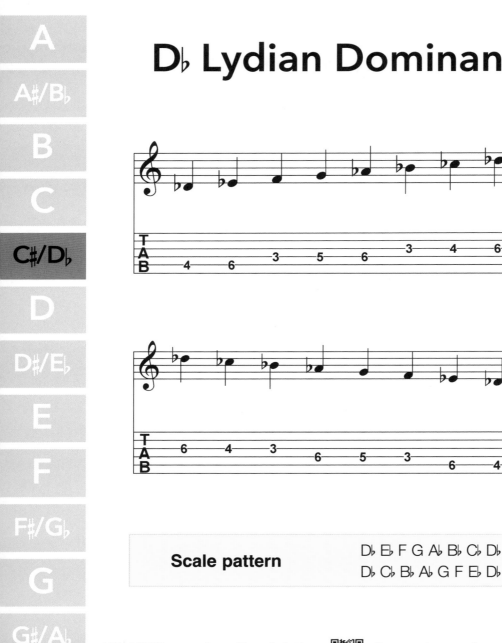

Scale pattern	D♭ E♭ F G A♭ B♭ C♭ D♭	
	D♭ C♭ B♭ A♭ G F E♭ D♭	

FREE ACCESS on smartphones, iPhone, Android etc. Use any QR code app to scan this QR code

Or go straight to www.flametreemusic.com to **HEAR** chords, scales, and find more resources

108

A
A♯/B♭
B
C
C♯/D♭
D
D♯/E♭
E
F
F♯/G♭
G
G♯/A♭

C♯ Diminished

| Scale pattern | C♯ D E F G G♯ A♯ B C♯ |
| | C♯ B A♯ G♯ G♭ F E D C♯ |

A

A♯/B♭

B

C

C♯/D♭

D

D♯/E♭

E

F

F♯/G♭

G

G♯/A♭

C♯ Chromatic

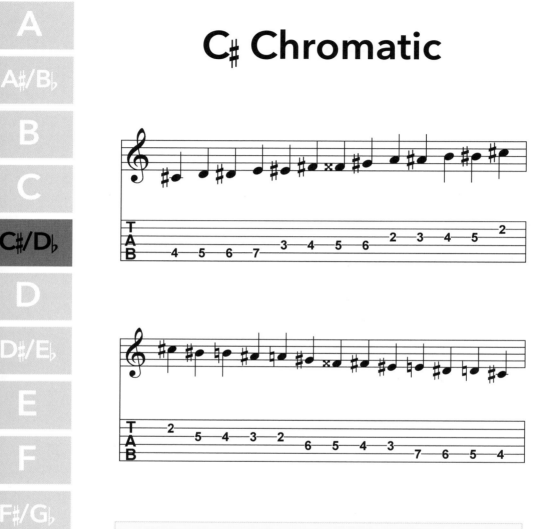

A
A♯/B♭
B
C
C♯/D♭
D
D♯/E♭
E
F
F♯/G♭
G
G♯/A♭

Scale pattern

C♯ D D♯ E E♯ F♯ F𝄪 G♯ A A♯ B B♯ C♯
C♯ B♯ B♮ A♯ A♮ G♯ F𝄪 F♯ E♯ E♮ D♯ D♮ C♯

C♯ Wholetone

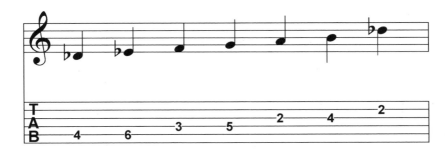

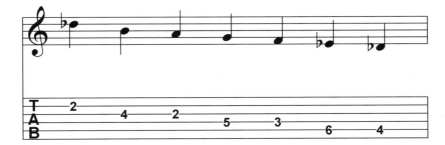

Scale pattern	D♭ E♭ F G A B D♭
	D♭ B A G F E♭ D♭

A

A♯/B♭

B

C

C♯/D♭

D

D♯/E♭

E

F

F♯/G♭

G

G♯/A♭

FREE ACCESS on smartphones, iPhone, Android etc.
Use any QR code app to scan this QR code

Or go straight to www.flametreemusic.com to
HEAR chords, scales, and find more resources

SCALES
& MODES

D

A
A♯/B♭
B
C
C♯/D♭
D
D♯/E♭
E
F
F♯/G♭
G
G♯/A♭

FREE ACCESS on smartphones, iPhone, Android etc. Use any QR code app to scan this QR code

Or go straight to www.flametreemusic.com to **HEAR** chords, scales, and find more resources

D Major

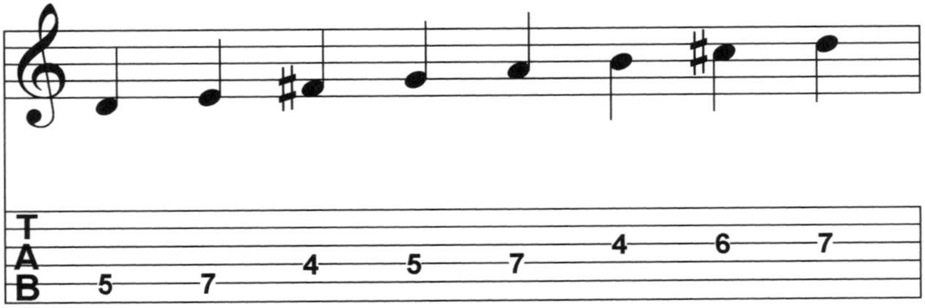

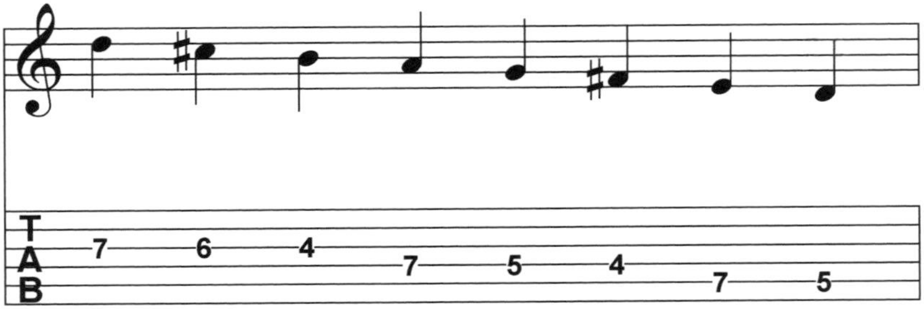

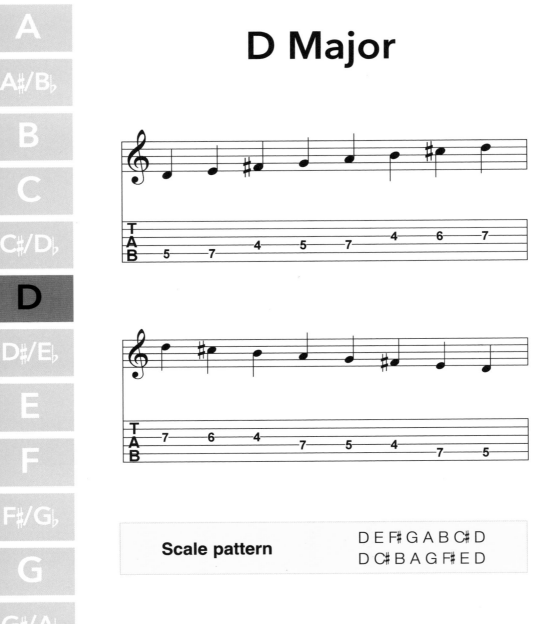

Scale pattern	D E F♯ G A B C♯ D D C♯ B A G F♯ E D

D Major Pentatonic

Scale pattern	D E F♯ A B D
	D B A F♯ E D

A
A♯/B♭
B
C
C♯/D♭
D
D♯/E♭
E
F
F♯/G♭
G
G♯/A♭

Or go straight to www.flametreemusic.com to **HEAR** chords, scales, and find more resources

D Lydian

Scale pattern	D E F# G# A B C# D
	D C# B A G# F# E D

FREE ACCESS on smartphones, iPhone, Android etc.
Use any QR code app to scan this QR code

Or go straight to www.flametreemusic.com to
HEAR chords, scales, and find more resources

D Lydian Augmented

| Scale pattern | D E F# G# A# B C# D |
| | D C# B A# G# F# E D |

FREE ACCESS on smartphones, iPhone, Android etc.
Use any QR code app to scan this QR code

Or go straight to www.flametreemusic.com to
HEAR chords, scales, and find more resources

A
A#/B♭
B
C
C#/D♭
D
D#/E♭
E
F
F#/G♭
G
G#/A♭

D Natural Minor

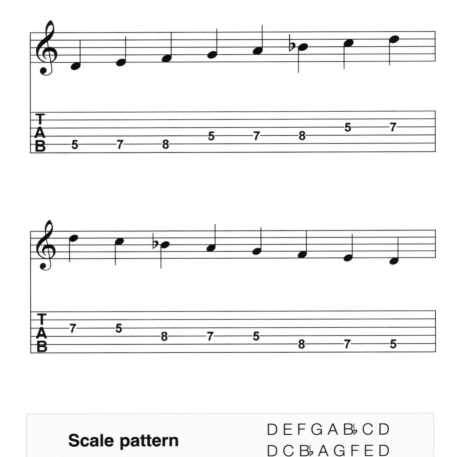

Scale pattern	D E F G A B♭ C D
	D C B♭ A G F E D

FREE ACCESS on smartphones, iPhone, Android etc.
Use any QR code app to scan this QR code

Or go straight to www.flametreemusic.com to
HEAR chords, scales, and find more resources

D Harmonic Minor

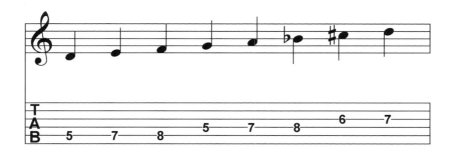

Scale pattern	D E F G A B♭ C♯ D
	D C♯ B♭ A G F E D

119

D Melodic Minor

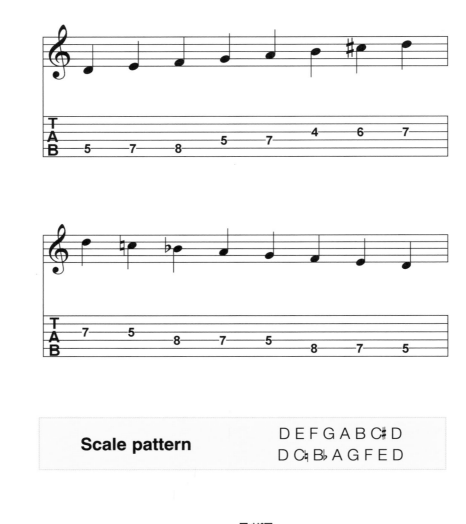

Scale pattern

D E F G A B C♯ D
D C♮ B♭ A G F E D

FREE ACCESS on smartphones, iPhone, Android etc.
Use any QR code app to scan this QR code

Or go straight to www.flametreemusic.com to
HEAR chords, scales, and find more resources

D Dorian

Scale pattern	D E F G A B C D
	D C B A G F E D

A
A#/B♭
B
C
C#/D♭
D
D#/E♭
E
F
F#/G♭
G
G#/A♭

D Minor Pentatonic

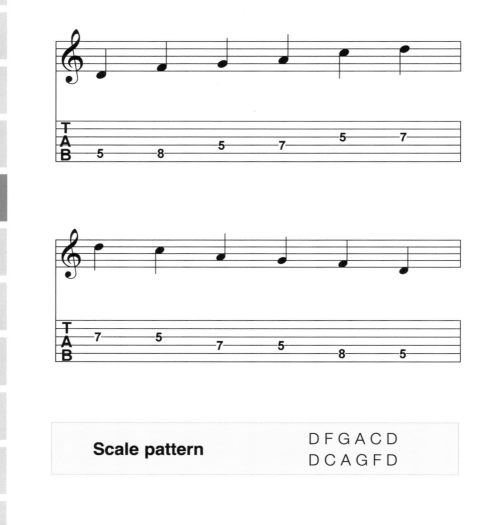

Scale pattern	D F G A C D D C A G F D

FREE ACCESS on smartphones, iPhone, Android etc.
Use any QR code app to scan this QR code

Or go straight to www.flametreemusic.com to
HEAR chords, scales, and find more resources

122

D Blues

Scale pattern

D F G A♭ A♮ C D
D C A♮ A♭ G F D

A

A♯/B♭

B

C

C♯/D♭

D

D♯/E♭

E

F

F♯/G♭

G

G♯/A♭

D Phrygian

Scale pattern

D E♭ F G A B♭ C D
D C B♭ A G F E♭ D

FREE ACCESS on smartphones, iPhone, Android etc.
Use any QR code app to scan this QR code

Or go straight to www.flametreemusic.com to
HEAR chords, scales, and find more resources

124

D Locrian

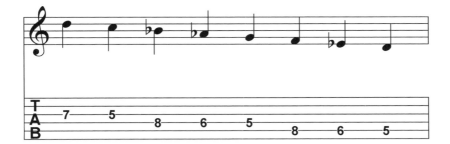

Scale pattern

D E♭ F G A♭ B♭ C D
D C B♭ A♭ G F E♭ D

A
A#/B♭
B
C
C#/D♭
D
D#/E♭
E
F
F#/G♭
G
G#/A♭

D Mixolydian

Scale pattern

D E F♯ G A B C D
D C B A G F♯ E D

Or go straight to www.flametreemusic.com to **HEAR** chords, scales, and find more resources

A
A♯/B♭
B
C
C♯/D♭
D
D♯/E♭
E
F
F♯/G♭
G
G♯/A♭

D Phrygian Major
(Spanish Gypsy)

Scale pattern	D E♭ F♯ G A B♭ C D
	D C B♭ A G F♯ E♭ D

A

A♯/B♭

B

C

C♯/D♭

D

D♯/E♭

E

F

F♯/G♭

G

G♯/A♭

D Lydian Dominant

Scale pattern	D E F# G# A B C D
	D C B A G# F# E D

D Diminished

A
A♯/B♭
B
C
C♯/D♭
D
D♯/E♭
E
F
F♯/G♭
G
G♯/A♭

Scale pattern

D E♭ F F♯ G♯ A B C D
D C B A G♯ F♯ F♮ E♭ D

FREE ACCESS on smartphones, iPhone, Android etc.
Use any QR code app to scan this QR code

Or go straight to www.flametreemusic.com to
HEAR chords, scales, and find more resources

129

D Chromatic

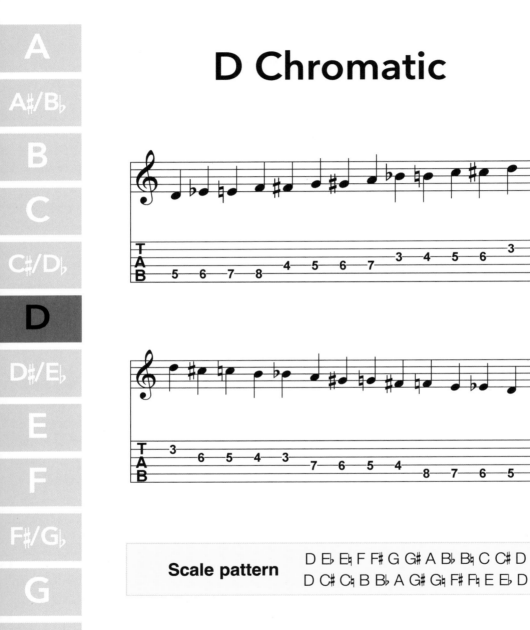

Scale pattern
D E♭ E♮ F F♯ G G♯ A B♭ B♮ C C♯ D
D C♯ C♮ B B♭ A G♯ G♮ F♯ F♮ E E♭ D

Or go straight to www.flametreemusic.com to
HEAR chords, scales, and find more resources

D Wholetone

Scale pattern	D E F# G# A# C D
	D C A# G# F# E D

A

A#/B♭

B

C

C#/D♭

D

D#/E♭

E

F

F#/G♭

G

G#/A♭

SCALES
& MODES

D#
E♭

A

A#/B♭

B

C

C#/D♭

D

D#/E♭

E

F

F#/G♭

G

G#/A♭

FREE ACCESS on smartphones, iPhone, Android etc.
Use any QR code app to scan this QR code

Or go straight to www.flametreemusic.com to
HEAR chords, scales, and find more resources

E♭ Major

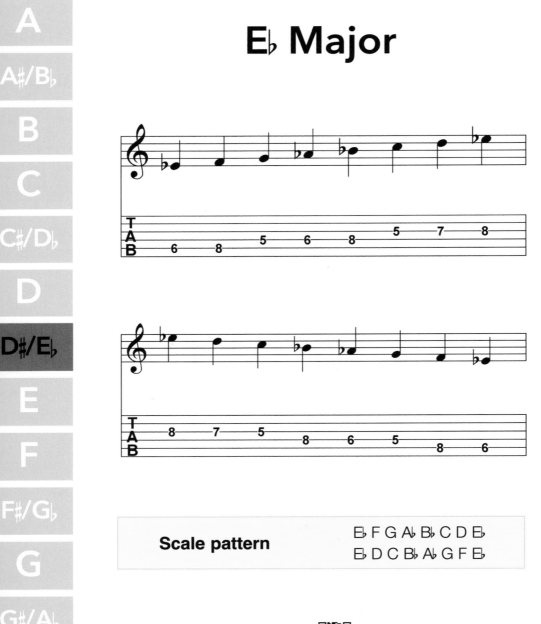

Scale pattern

E♭ F G A♭ B♭ C D E♭
E♭ D C B♭ A♭ G F E♭

E♭ Major Pentatonic

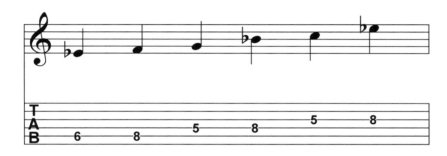

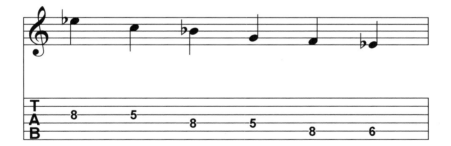

Scale pattern	E♭ F G B♭ C E♭
	E♭ C B♭ G F E♭

Or go straight to www.flametreemusic.com to
HEAR chords, scales, and find more resources

E♭ Lydian

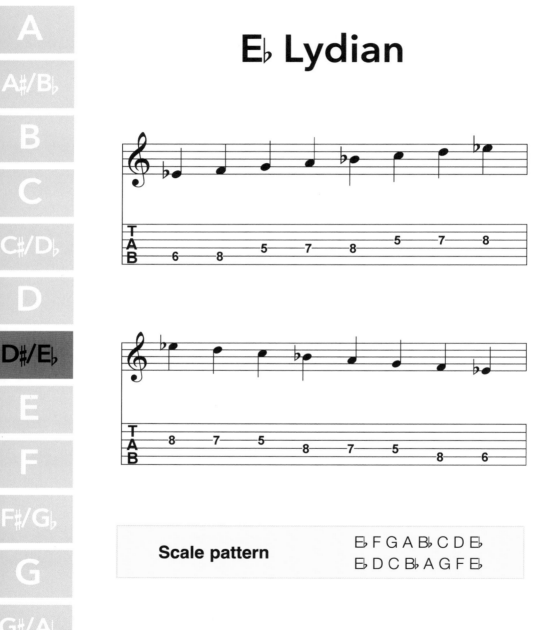

Scale pattern	E♭ F G A B♭ C D E♭
	E♭ D C B♭ A G F E♭

FREE ACCESS on smartphones, iPhone, Android etc. Use any QR code app to scan this QR code

Or go straight to www.flametreemusic.com to **HEAR** chords, scales, and find more resources

136

E♭ Lydian Augmented

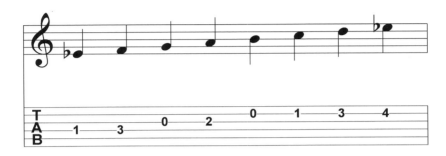

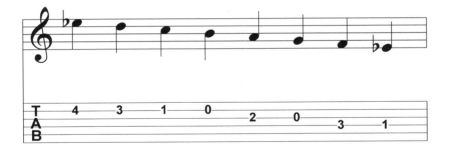

Scale pattern	E♭ F G A B C D E♭
	E♭ D C B A G F E♭

A

A♯/B♭

B

C

C♯/D♭

D

D♯/E♭

E

F

F♯/G♭

G

G♯/A♭

E♭ Natural Minor

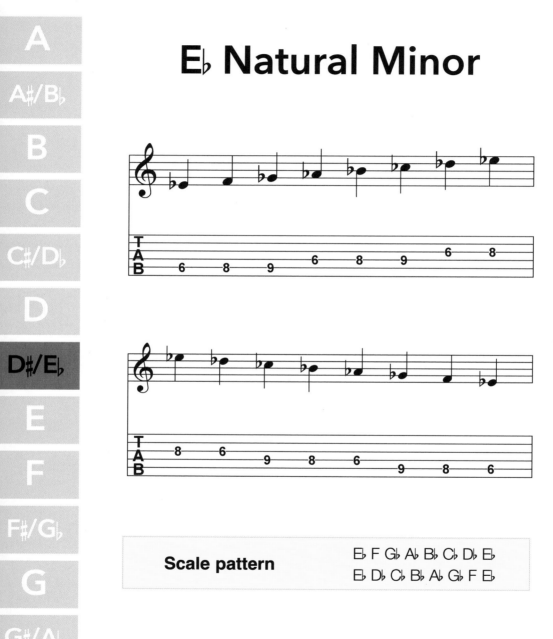

Scale pattern	E♭ F G♭ A♭ B♭ C♭ D♭ E♭
	E♭ D♭ C♭ B♭ A♭ G♭ F E♭

FREE ACCESS on smartphones, iPhone, Android etc.
Use any QR code app to scan this QR code

Or go straight to www.flametreemusic.com to
HEAR chords, scales, and find more resources

E♭ Harmonic Minor

A
A#/B♭
B
C
C#/D♭
D
D#/E♭
E
F
F#/G♭
G
G#/A♭

Scale pattern	E♭ F G♭ A♭ B♭ C♭ D E♭
	E♭ D C♭ B♭ A♭ G♭ F E♭

FREE ACCESS on smartphones, iPhone, Android etc.
Use any QR code app to scan this QR code

Or go straight to www.flametreemusic.com to
HEAR chords, scales, and find more resources

139

E♭ Melodic Minor

Scale pattern

E♭ F G♭ A♭ B♭ C D E♭
E♭ D♭ C♭ B♭ A♭ G♭ F E♭

Or go straight to www.flametreemusic.com to **HEAR** chords, scales, and find more resources

E♭ Dorian

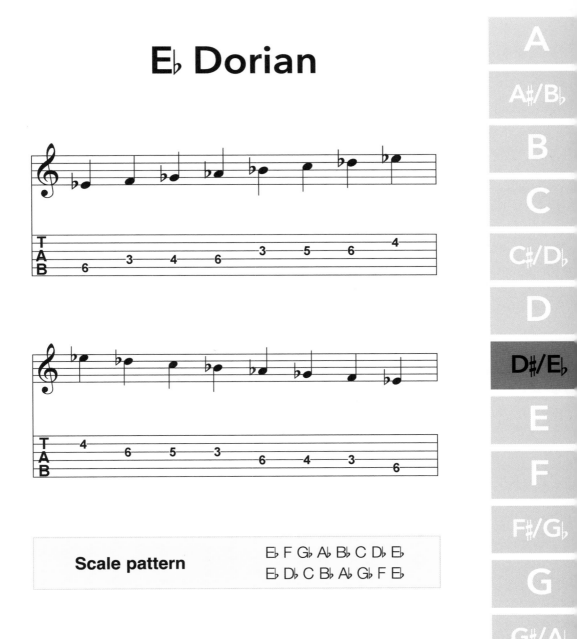

Scale pattern	E♭ F G♭ A♭ B♭ C D♭ E♭
	E♭ D♭ C B♭ A♭ G♭ F E♭

Or go straight to www.flametreemusic.com to **HEAR** chords, scales, and find more resources

A

A♯/B♭

B

C

C♯/D♭

D

D♯/E♭

E

F

F♯/G♭

G

G♯/A♭

E♭ Minor Pentatonic

Scale pattern

E♭ G♭ A♭ B♭ D♭ E♭
E♭ D♭ B♭ A♭ G♭ E♭

Or go straight to www.flametreemusic.com to
HEAR chords, scales, and find more resources

D♯ Blues

Scale pattern	D♯ F♯ G♯ A♮ A♯ C♯ D♯
	D♯ C♯ A♯ A♮ G♯ F♯ D♯

FREE ACCESS on smartphones, iPhone, Android etc.
Use any QR code app to scan this QR code

Or go straight to www.flametreemusic.com to
HEAR chords, scales, and find more resources

D# Phrygian

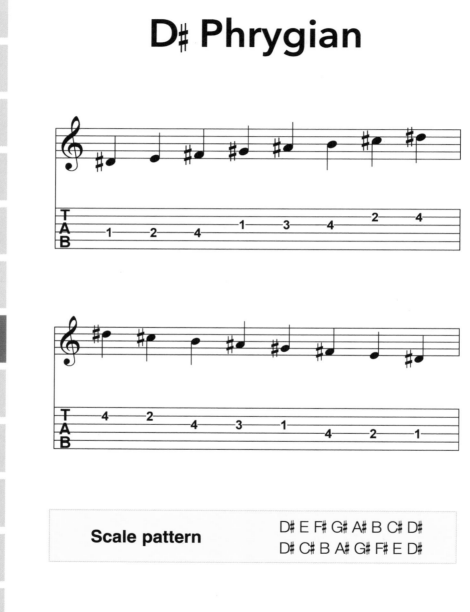

Scale pattern	D# E F# G# A# B C# D#
	D# C# B A# G# F# E D#

FREE ACCESS on smartphones, iPhone, Android etc.
Use any QR code app to scan this QR code

Or go straight to www.flametreemusic.com to
HEAR chords, scales, and find more resources

144

D♯ Locrian

| A |
| A♯/B♭ |
| B |
| C |
| C♯/D♭ |
| D |
| D♯/E♭ |
| E |
| F |
| F♯/G♭ |
| G |
| G♯/A♭ |

Scale pattern	D♯ E F♯ G♯ A B C♯ D♯
	D♯ C♯ B A G♯ F♯ E D♯

Or go straight to www.flametreemusic.com to **HEAR** chords, scales, and find more resources

E♭ Mixolydian

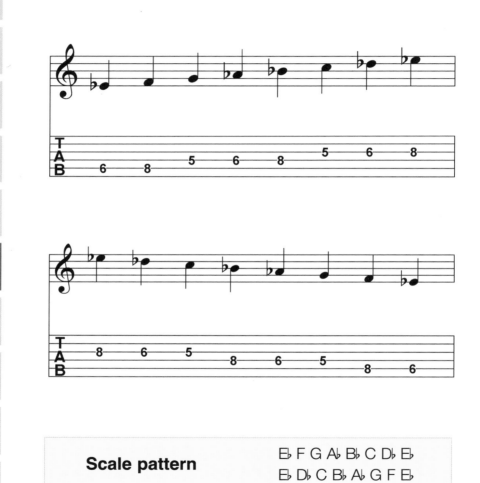

Scale pattern	E♭ F G A♭ B♭ C D♭ E♭
	E♭ D♭ C B♭ A♭ G F E♭

Or go straight to www.flametreemusic.com to
HEAR chords, scales, and find more resources

E♭ Phrygian Major
(Spanish Gypsy)

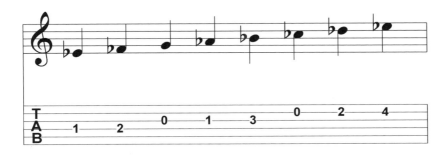

Scale pattern	E♭ F♭ G A♭ B♭ C♭ D♭ E♭
	E♭ D♭ C♭ B♭ A♭ G F♭ E♭

A

A♯/B♭

B

C

C♯/D♭

D

D♯/E♭

E

F

F♯/G♭

G

G♯/A♭

E♭ Lydian Dominant

Scale pattern	E♭ F G A B♭ C D♭ E♭
	E♭ D♭ C B♭ A G F E♭

E♭ Diminished

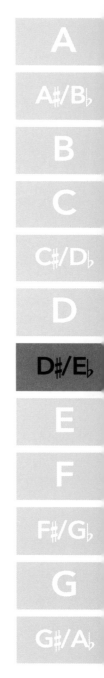

A

A♯/B♭

B

C

C♯/D♭

D

D♯/E♭

E

F

F♯/G♭

G

G♯/A♭

Scale pattern

E♭ F♭ G♭ G♮ A B♭ C D♭ E♭
E♭ D♭ C B♭ A G G♭ F♭ E♭

Or go straight to www.flametreemusic.com to **HEAR** chords, scales, and find more resources

E♭ Chromatic

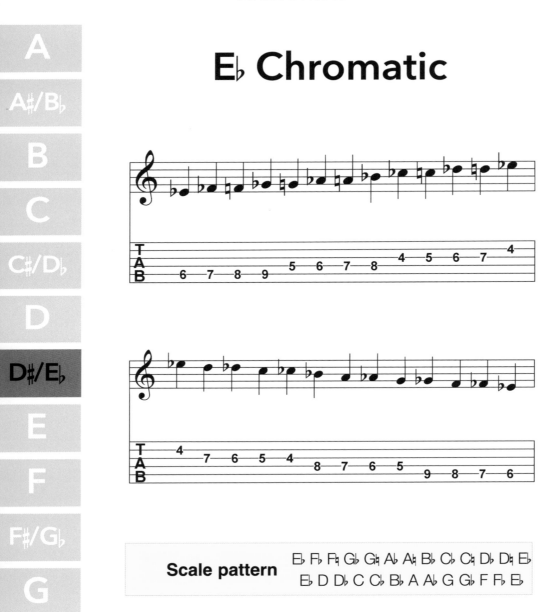

Scale pattern

E♭ F♭ F♮ G♭ G♮ A♭ A♮ B♭ C♭ C♮ D♭ D♮ E♭
E♭ D D♭ C C♭ B♭ A A♭ G G♭ F F♭ E♭

E♭ Wholetone

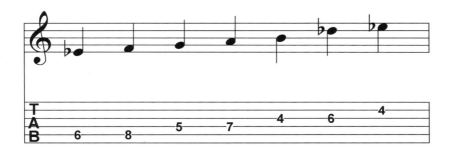

Scale pattern

E♭ F G A B D♭ E♭
E♭ D♭ B A G F E♭

Or go straight to www.flametreemusic.com to
HEAR chords, scales, and find more resources

A
A♯/B♭
B
C
C♯/D♭
D
D♯/E♭
E
F
F♯/G♭
G
G♯/A♭

SCALES
& MODES

E

A

A#/B♭

B

C

C#/D♭

D

D#/E♭

E

F

F#/G♭

G

G#/A♭

FREE ACCESS on smartphones, iPhone, Android etc.
Use any QR code app to scan this QR code

Or go straight to www.flametreemusic.com to
HEAR chords, scales, and find more resources

153

E Major

Scale pattern	E F♯ G♯ A B C♯ D♯ E
	E D♯ C♯ B A G♯ F♯ E

E Major Pentatonic

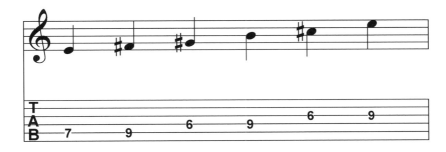

Scale pattern	E F# G# B C# E
	E C# B G# F# E

A

A#/B♭

B

C

C#/D♭

D

D#/E♭

E

F

F#/G♭

G

G#/A♭

E Lydian

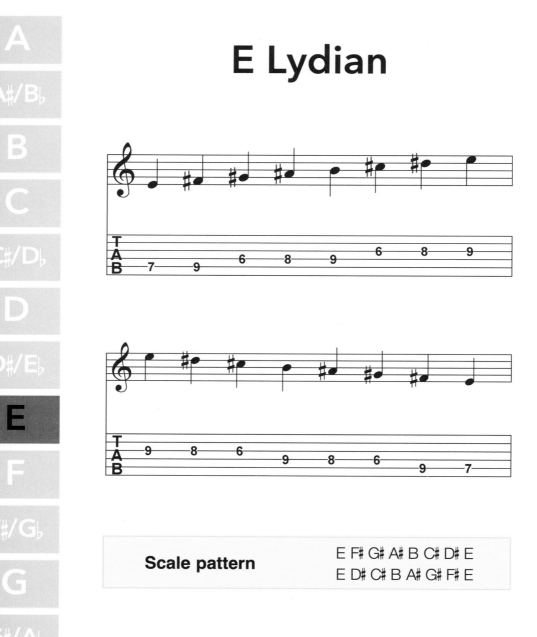

Scale pattern	E F# G# A# B C# D# E
	E D# C# B A# G# F# E

FREE ACCESS on smartphones, iPhone, Android etc.
Use any QR code app to scan this QR code

Or go straight to www.flametreemusic.com to
HEAR chords, scales, and find more resources

E Lydian Augmented

Scale pattern	E F# G# A# B# C# D# E
	E D# C# B# A# G# F# E

FREE ACCESS on smartphones, iPhone, Android etc.
Use any QR code app to scan this QR code

Or go straight to www.flametreemusic.com to
HEAR chords, scales, and find more resources

157

E Natural Minor

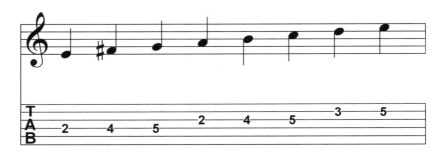

Scale pattern	E F# G A B C D E E D C B A G F# E

FREE ACCESS on smartphones, iPhone, Android etc.
Use any QR code app to scan this QR code

Or go straight to www.flametreemusic.com to
HEAR chords, scales, and find more resources

E Harmonic Minor

| **Scale pattern** | E F♯ G A B C D♯ E |
| | E D♯ C B A G F♯ E |

FREE ACCESS on smartphones, iPhone, Android etc.
Use any QR code app to scan this QR code

Or go straight to www.flametreemusic.com to
HEAR chords, scales, and find more resources

E Melodic Minor

Scale pattern

E F# G A B C# D# E
E D♮ C♮ B A G F# E

FREE ACCESS on smartphones, iPhone, Android etc.
Use any QR code app to scan this QR code

Or go straight to www.flametreemusic.com to
HEAR chords, scales, and find more resources

E Dorian

Scale pattern	E F♯ G A B C D♯ E
	E D C♯ B A G F♯ E

FREE ACCESS on smartphones, iPhone, Android etc.
Use any QR code app to scan this QR code

Or go straight to www.flametreemusic.com to
HEAR chords, scales, and find more resources

A
A♯/B♭
B
C
C♯/D♭
D
D♯/E♭
E
F
F♯/G♭
G
G♯/A♭

E Minor Pentatonic

| **Scale pattern** | E G A B D E |
| | E D B A G E |

FREE ACCESS on smartphones, iPhone, Android etc.
Use any QR code app to scan this QR code

Or go straight to www.flametreemusic.com to
HEAR chords, scales, and find more resources

162

E Blues

Scale pattern	E G A B♭ B♮ D E
	E D B♮ B♭ A G E

A
A♯/B♭
B
C
C♯/D♭
D
D♯/E♭
E
F
F♯/G♭
G
G♯/A♭

FREE ACCESS on smartphones, iPhone, Android etc. Use any QR code app to scan this QR code

Or go straight to www.flametreemusic.com to **HEAR** chords, scales, and find more resources

163

E Phrygian

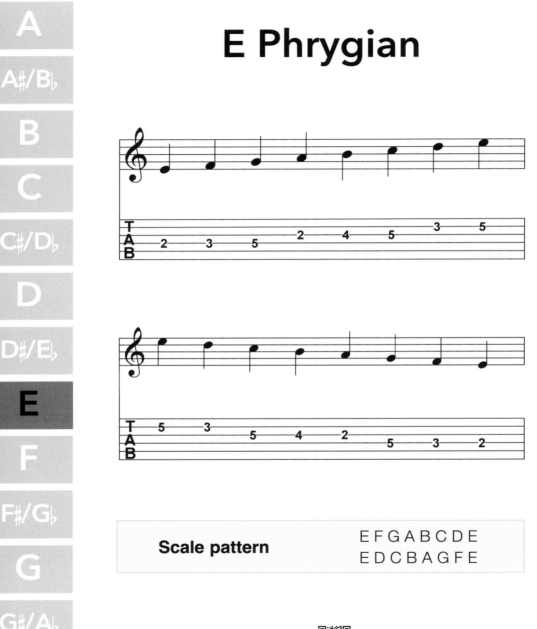

| Scale pattern | E F G A B C D E |
| | E D C B A G F E |

FREE ACCESS on smartphones, iPhone, Android etc. Use any QR code app to scan this QR code

Or go straight to www.flametreemusic.com to **HEAR** chords, scales, and find more resources

164

E Locrian

Scale pattern	E F G A B♭ C D E		
	E D C B♭ A G F E		

Or go straight to www.flametreemusic.com to
HEAR chords, scales, and find more resources

A
A♯/B♭
B
C
C♯/D♭
D
D♯/E♭
E
F
F♯/G♭
G
G♯/A♭

E Mixolydian

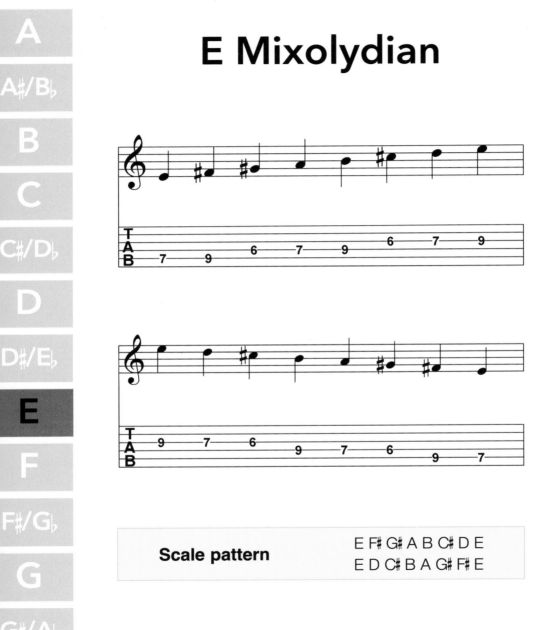

Scale pattern	E F# G# A B C# D E
	E D C# B A G# F# E

FREE ACCESS on smartphones, iPhone, Android etc.
Use any QR code app to scan this QR code

Or go straight to www.flametreemusic.com to
HEAR chords, scales, and find more resources

166

E Phrygian Major
(Spanish Gypsy)

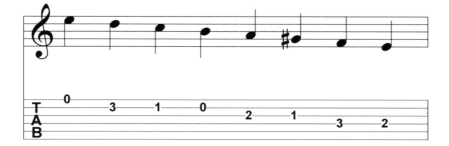

Scale pattern	E F G# A B C D E
	E D C B A G# F E

A

A#/B♭

B

C

C#/D♭

D

D#/E♭

E

F

F#/G♭

G

G#/A♭

E Lydian Dominant

Scale pattern	E F# G# A# B C# D E
	E D C# B A# G# F# E

E Diminished

Scale pattern	E F G G# A# B C# D E
	E D C# B A# G# G♮ F E

A

A#/B♭

B

C

C#/D♭

D

D#/E♭

E

F

F#/G♭

G

G#/A♭

FREE ACCESS on smartphones, iPhone, Android etc. Use any QR code app to scan this QR code

Or go straight to www.flametreemusic.com to **HEAR** chords, scales, and find more resources

169

E Chromatic

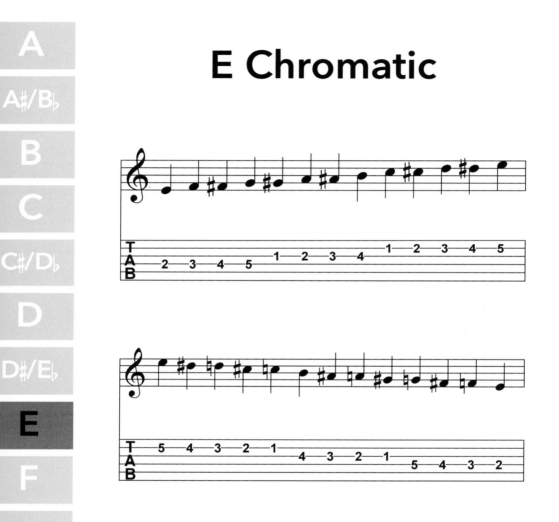

Scale pattern

E F F# G G# A A# B C C# D D# E
E D# D♭ C# C♮ B A# A♮ G# G♮ F# F♮ E

FREE ACCESS on smartphones, iPhone, Android etc.
Use any QR code app to scan this QR code

Or go straight to www.flametreemusic.com to
HEAR chords, scales, and find more resources

E Wholetone

Scale pattern	E F♯ G♯ A♯ C D E
	E D C A♯ G♯ F♯ E

FREE ACCESS on smartphones, iPhone, Android etc.
Use any QR code app to scan this QR code

Or go straight to www.flametreemusic.com to
HEAR chords, scales, and find more resources

A

A♯/B♭

B

C

C♯/D♭

D

D♯/E♭

E

F

F♯/G♭

G

G♯/A♭

SCALES
& MODES

F

FREE ACCESS on smartphones, iPhone, Android etc.
Use any QR code app to scan this QR code

Or go straight to www.flametreemusic.com to
HEAR chords, scales, and find more resources

A

A#/B♭

B

C

C#/D♭

D

D#/E♭

E

F

F#/G♭

G

G#/A♭

F Major

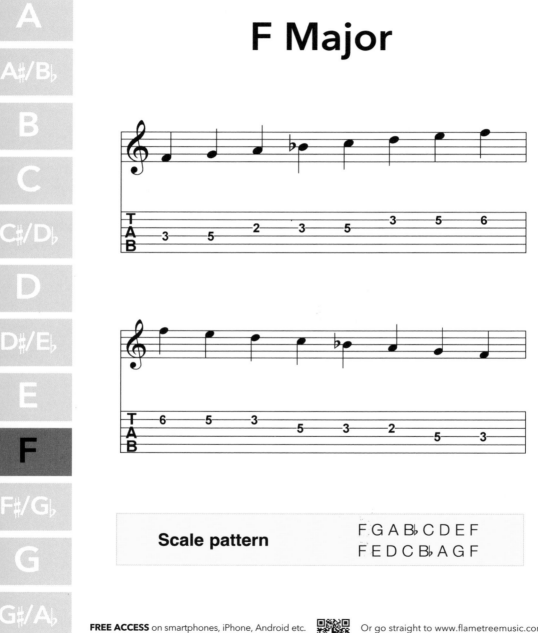

Scale pattern	F G A B♭ C D E F
	F E D C B♭ A G F

F Major Pentatonic

Scale pattern	F G A C D F
	F D C A G F

Or go straight to www.flametreemusic.com to
HEAR chords, scales, and find more resources

F Lydian

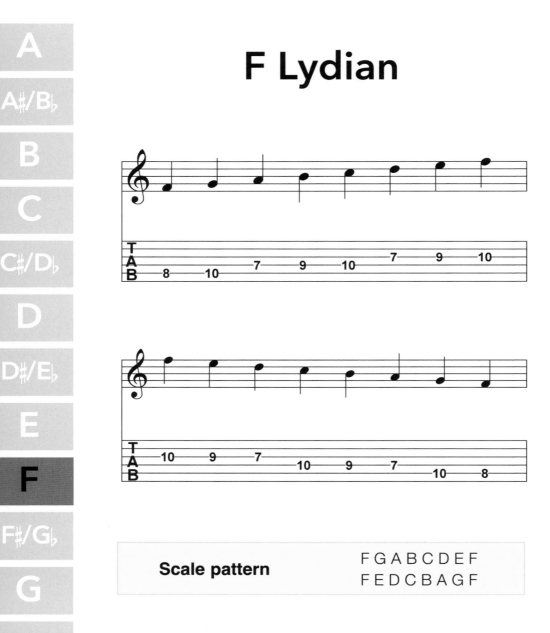

Scale pattern	F G A B C D E F
	F E D C B A G F

FREE ACCESS on smartphones, iPhone, Android etc.
Use any QR code app to scan this QR code

Or go straight to www.flametreemusic.com to
HEAR chords, scales, and find more resources

F Lydian Augmented

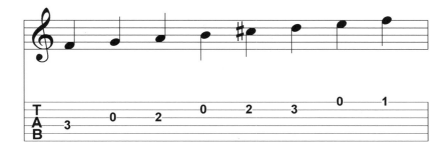

Scale pattern	F G A B C♯ D E F
	F E D C♯ B A G F

A
A♯/B♭
B
C
C♯/D♭
D
D♯/E♭
E
F
F♯/G♭
G
G♯/A♭

FREE ACCESS on smartphones, iPhone, Android etc. Use any QR code app to scan this QR code

Or go straight to www.flametreemusic.com to **HEAR** chords, scales, and find more resources

177

F Natural Minor

Scale pattern

F G A♭ B♭ C D♭ E♭ F
F E♭ D♭ C B♭ A♭ G F

Or go straight to www.flametreemusic.com to
HEAR chords, scales, and find more resources

F Harmonic Minor

Scale pattern	F G A♭ B♭ C D♭ E F
	F E D♭ C B♭ A♭ G F

A

A#/B♭

B

C

C#/D♭

D

D#/E♭

E

F

F#/G♭

G

G#/A♭

FREE ACCESS on smartphones, iPhone, Android etc.
Use any QR code app to scan this QR code

179

Or go straight to www.flametreemusic.com to
HEAR chords, scales, and find more resources

F Melodic Minor

| **Scale pattern** | F G A♭ B♭ C D E F |
| | F E♭ D♭ C B♭ A♭ G F |

FREE ACCESS on smartphones, iPhone, Android etc.
Use any QR code app to scan this QR code

Or go straight to www.flametreemusic.com to
HEAR chords, scales, and find more resources

180

F Dorian

Scale pattern

F G A♭ B♭ C D E♭ F
F E♭ D C B♭ A♭ G F

A

A♯/B♭

B

C

C♯/D♭

D

D♯/E♭

E

F

F♯/G♭

G

G♯/A♭

F Minor Pentatonic

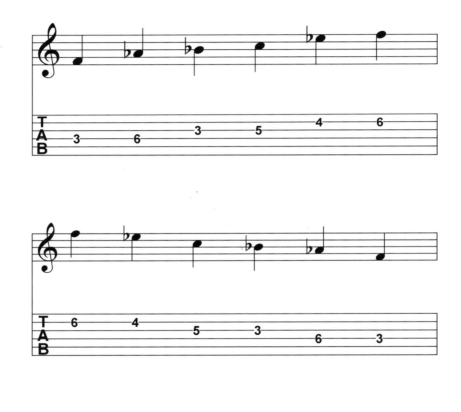

Scale pattern	F A♭ B♭ C E♭ F
	F E♭ C B♭ A♭ F

F Blues

| **Scale pattern** | F A♭ B♭ C♭ C♮ E♭ F |
| | F E♭ C♮ C♭ B♭ A♭ F |

Or go straight to www.flametreemusic.com to
HEAR chords, scales, and find more resources

A

A♯/B♭

B

C

C♯/D♭

D

D♯/E♭

E

F

F♯/G♭

G

G♯/A♭

F Phrygian

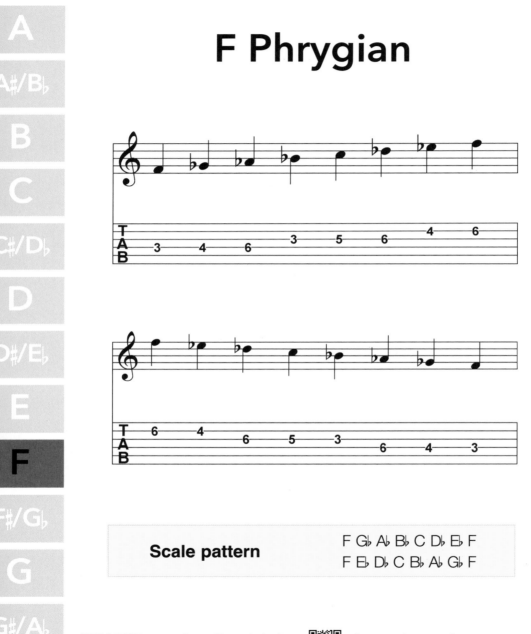

Scale pattern

F Gb Ab Bb C Db Eb F
F Eb Db C Bb Ab Gb F

FREE ACCESS on smartphones, iPhone, Android etc. Use any QR code app to scan this QR code

Or go straight to www.flametreemusic.com to **HEAR** chords, scales, and find more resources

F Locrian

Scale pattern	F G♭ A♭ B♭ C♭ D♭ E♭ F
	F E♭ D♭ C♭ B♭ A♭ G♭ F

A

A#/B♭

B

C

C#/D♭

D

D#/E♭

E

F

F#/G♭

G

G#/A♭

FREE ACCESS on smartphones, iPhone, Android etc.
Use any QR code app to scan this QR code

Or go straight to www.flametreemusic.com to
HEAR chords, scales, and find more resources

185

F Mixolydian

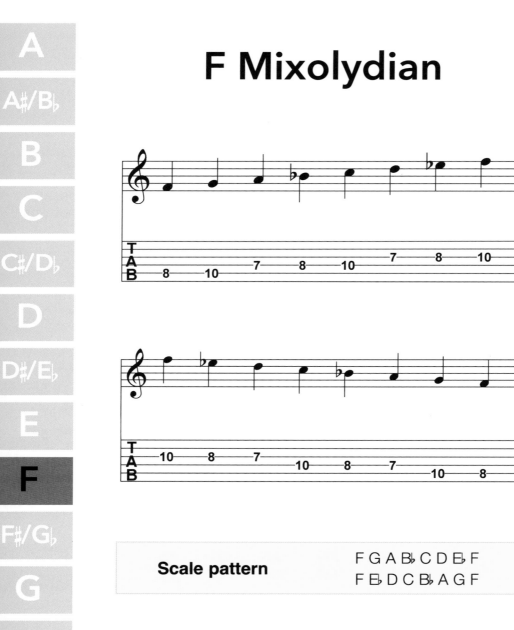

Scale pattern	F G A B♭ C D E♭ F
	F E♭ D C B♭ A G F

A
A#/B♭
B
C
C#/D♭
D
D#/E♭
E
F
F#/G♭
G
G#/A♭

F Phrygian Major
(Spanish Gypsy)

A
A♯/B♭
B
C
C♯/D♭
D
D♯/E♭
E
F
F♯/G♭
G
G♯/A♭

Scale pattern	F G♭ A B♭ C D♭ E♭ F
	F E♭ D♭ C B♭ A G♭ F

FREE ACCESS on smartphones, iPhone, Android etc.
Use any QR code app to scan this QR code

Or go straight to www.flametreemusic.com to
HEAR chords, scales, and find more resources

187

F Lydian Dominant

Scale pattern

F G A B C D E♭ F
F E♭ D C B A G F

FREE ACCESS on smartphones, iPhone, Android etc.
Use any QR code app to scan this QR code

Or go straight to www.flametreemusic.com to
HEAR chords, scales, and find more resources

188

F Diminished

A
A♯/B♭
B
C
C♯/D♭
D
D♯/E♭
E
F
F♯/G♭
G
G♯/A♭

Scale pattern

F G♭ A♭ A♮ B C D E♭ F
F E♭ D C B A A♭ G♭ F

FREE ACCESS on smartphones, iPhone, Android etc.
Use any QR code app to scan this QR code

Or go straight to www.flametreemusic.com to
HEAR chords, scales, and find more resources

F Chromatic

Scale pattern

F G♭ G♮ A♭ A♮ B♭ B♮ C D♭ D♮ E♭ E♮ F
F E E♭ D D♭ C B B♭ A A♭ G G♭ F

FREE ACCESS on smartphones, iPhone, Android etc.
Use any QR code app to scan this QR code

Or go straight to www.flametreemusic.com to
HEAR chords, scales, and find more resources

A
A#/B♭
B
C
C#/D♭
D
D#/E♭
E
F
F#/G♭
G
G#/A♭

F Wholetone

Scale pattern	F G A B C♯ D♯ F
	F D♯ C♯ B A G F

A
A♯/B♭
B
C
C♯/D♭
D
D♯/E♭
E
F
F♯/G♭
G
G♯/A♭

SCALES
& MODES

F# / Gb

A

A#/Bb

B

C

C#/Db

D

D#/Eb

E

F

F#/Gb

G

G#/Ab

F♯ Major

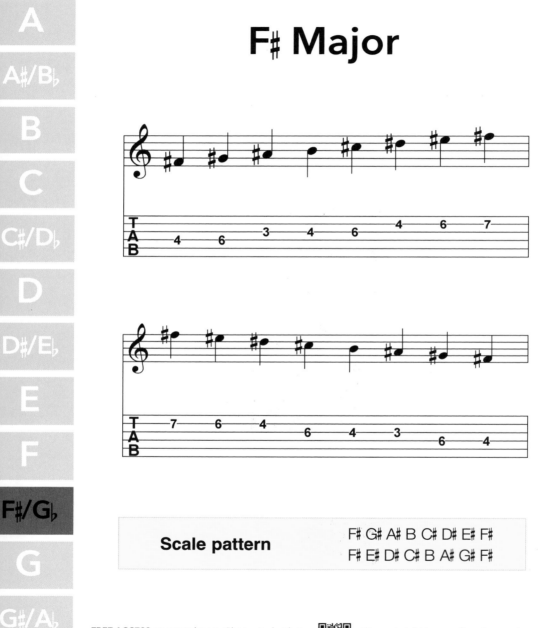

Scale pattern	F♯ G♯ A♯ B C♯ D♯ E♯ F♯
	F♯ E♯ D♯ C♯ B A♯ G♯ F♯

Or go straight to www.flametreemusic.com to
HEAR chords, scales, and find more resources

A
A♯/B♭
B
C
C♯/D♭
D
D♯/E♭
E
F
F♯/G♭
G
G♯/A♭

F♯ Major Pentatonic

Scale pattern

F♯ G♯ A♯ C♯ D♯ F♯

F♯ D♯ C♯ A♯ G♯ F♯

A
A♯/B♭
B
C
C♯/D♭
D
D♯/E♭
E
F
F♯/G♭
G
G♯/A♭

FREE ACCESS on smartphones, iPhone, Android etc.
Use any QR code app to scan this QR code

Or go straight to www.flametreemusic.com to
HEAR chords, scales, and find more resources

G♭ Lydian

Scale pattern	G♭ A♭ B♭ C D♭ E♭ F G♭
	G♭ F E♭ D♭ C B♭ A♭ G♭

Or go straight to www.flametreemusic.com to
HEAR chords, scales, and find more resources

A
A♯/B♭
B
C
C♯/D♭
D
D♯/E♭
E
F
F♯/G♭
G
G♯/A♭

G♭ Lydian Augmented

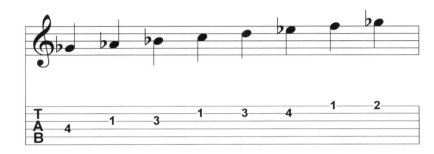

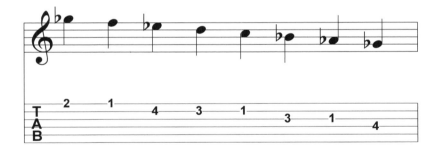

Scale pattern	G♭ A♭ B♭ C D E♭ F G♭
	G♭ F E♭ D C B♭ A♭ G♭

Or go straight to www.flametreemusic.com to
HEAR chords, scales, and find more resources

A
A♯/B♭
B
C
C♯/D♭
D
D♯/E♭
E
F
F♯/G♭
G
G♯/A♭

F# Natural Minor

Scale pattern	F# G# A B C# D E F#
	F# E D C# B A G# F#

Or go straight to www.flametreemusic.com to **HEAR** chords, scales, and find more resources

F# Harmonic Minor

Scale pattern	F# G# A B C# D E# F#
	F# E# D C# B A G# F#

FREE ACCESS on smartphones, iPhone, Android etc. Use any QR code app to scan this QR code

Or go straight to www.flametreemusic.com to **HEAR** chords, scales, and find more resources

A

A#/B♭

B

C

C#/D♭

D

D#/E♭

E

F

F#/G♭

G

G#/A♭

F♯ Melodic Minor

Scale pattern	F♯ G♯ A B C♯ D♯ E♯ F♯
	F♯ E♮ D♮ C♯ B A G♯ F♯

F# Dorian

Scale pattern	F# G# A B C# D# E F# F# E D# C# B A G# F#

A
A#/Bb
B
C
C#/Db
D
D#/Eb
E
F
F#/Gb
G
G#/Ab

F♯ Minor Pentatonic

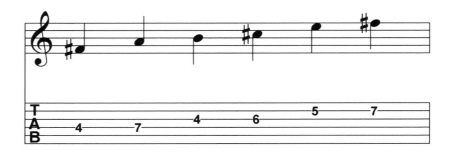

Scale pattern	F♯ A B C♯ E F♯
	F♯ E C♯ B A F♯

FREE ACCESS on smartphones, iPhone, Android etc.
Use any QR code app to scan this QR code

Or go straight to www.flametreemusic.com to
HEAR chords, scales, and find more resources

F♯ Blues

| Scale pattern | F♯ A B C♮ C♯ E F♯
F♯ E C♯ C♮ B A F♯ |

A
A♯/B♭
B
C
C♯/D♭
D
D♯/E♭
E
F
F♯/G♭
G
G♯/A♭

F♯ Phrygian

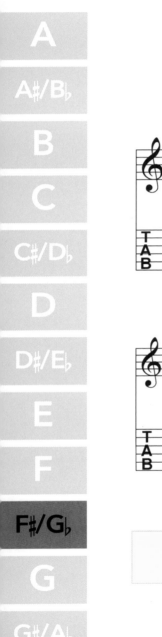

Scale pattern	F♯ G A B C♯ D E F♯
	F♯ E D C♯ B A G F♯

Or go straight to www.flametreemusic.com to **HEAR** chords, scales, and find more resources

F♯ Locrian

Scale pattern

F♯ G A B C D E F♯
F♯ E D C B A G F♯

A
A♯/B♭
B
C
C♯/D♭
D
D♯/E♭
E
F
F♯/G♭
G
G♯/A♭

Or go straight to www.flametreemusic.com to **HEAR** chords, scales, and find more resources

F♯ Mixolydian

Scale pattern	F♯ G♯ A♯ B C♯ D♯ E F♯
	F♯ E D♯ C♯ B A♯ G♯ F♯

Or go straight to www.flametreemusic.com to
HEAR chords, scales, and find more resources

F# Phrygian Major
(Spanish Gypsy)

Scale pattern	F# G A# B C# D E F# F# E D C# B A# G F#

Or go straight to www.flametreemusic.com to
HEAR chords, scales, and find more resources

A

A#/B♭

B

C

C#/D♭

D

D#/E♭

E

F

F#/G♭

G

G#/A♭

F# Lydian Dominant

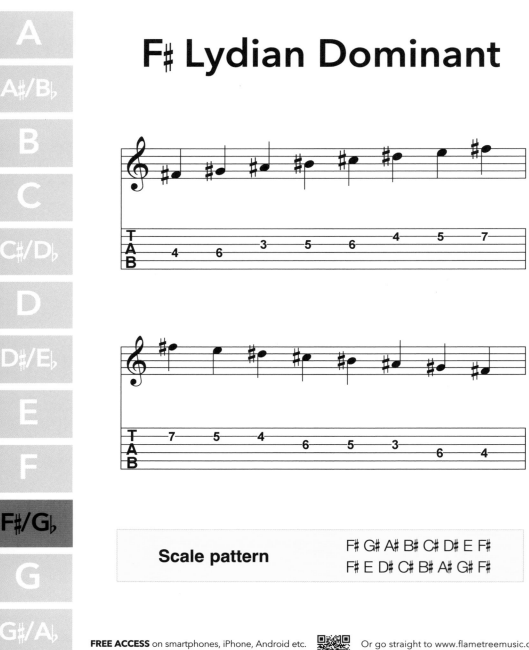

Scale pattern	F# G# A# B# C# D# E F#
	F# E D# C# B# A# G# F#

FREE ACCESS on smartphones, iPhone, Android etc.
Use any QR code app to scan this QR code

Or go straight to www.flametreemusic.com to
HEAR chords, scales, and find more resources

208

F♯ Diminished

Scale pattern	F♯ G A A♯ B♯ C♯ D♯ E F♯
	F♯ E D♯ C♯ B♯ A♯ A♮ G F♯

FREE ACCESS on smartphones, iPhone, Android etc.
Use any QR code app to scan this QR code

Or go straight to www.flametreemusic.com to
HEAR chords, scales, and find more resources

F# Chromatic

Scale pattern

F# G G# A A# B B# C# D D# E E# F#
F# E# E♮ D# D♮ C# B# B♮ A# A♮ G# G♮ F#

F♯ Wholetone

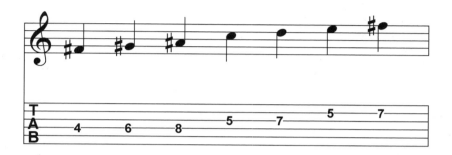

A
A♯/B♭
B
C
C♯/D♭
D
D♯/E♭
E
F
F♯/G♭
G
G♯/A♭

Scale pattern

F♯ G♯ A♯ C D E F♯
F♯ E D C A♯ G♯ F♯

FREE ACCESS on smartphones, iPhone, Android etc.
Use any QR code app to scan this QR code

Or go straight to www.flametreemusic.com to
HEAR chords, scales, and find more resources

211

SCALES & MODES

G

Or go straight to www.flametreemusic.com to
HEAR chords, scales, and find more resources

A

A#/B♭

B

C

C#/D♭

D

D#/E♭

E

F

F#/G♭

G

G#/A♭

G Major

| Scale pattern | G A B C D E F# G |
| | G F# E D C B A G |

Or go straight to www.flametreemusic.com to
HEAR chords, scales, and find more resources

A

A#/Bb

B

C

C#/Db

D

D#/Eb

E

F

F#/Gb

G

G#/Ab

G Major Pentatonic

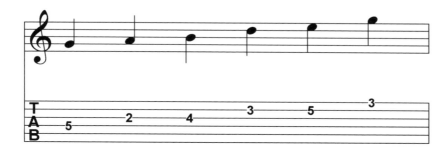

Scale pattern	G A B D E G
	G E D B A G

A
A#/B♭
B
C
C#/D♭
D
D#/E♭
E
F
F#/G♭
G
G#/A♭

G Lydian

Scale pattern	G A B C♯ D E F♯ G
	G F♯ E D C♯ B A G

A
A♯/B♭
B
C
C♯/D♭
D
D♯/E♭
E
F
F♯/G♭
G
G♯/A♭

G Lydian Augmented

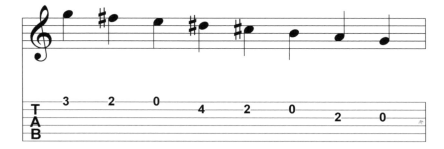

Scale pattern	G A B C# D# E F# G
	G F# E D# C# B A G

A

A#/Bb

B

C

C#/Db

D

D#/Eb

E

F

F#/Gb

G

G#/Ab

G Natural Minor

Scale pattern	G A B♭ C D E♭ F G
	G F E♭ D C B♭ A G

G Harmonic Minor

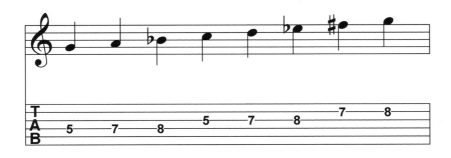

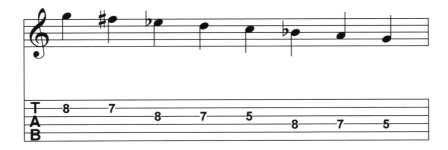

Scale pattern	G A B♭ C D E♭ F♯ G
	G F♯ E♭ D C B♭ A G

Or go straight to www.flametreemusic.com to
HEAR chords, scales, and find more resources

A

A♯/B♭

B

C

C♯/D♭

D

D♯/E♭

E

F

F♯/G♭

G

G♯/A♭

G Melodic Minor

Scale pattern

G A B♭ C D E F♯ G
G F♮ E♭ D C B♭ A G

FREE ACCESS on smartphones, iPhone, Android etc.
Use any QR code app to scan this QR code

Or go straight to www.flametreemusic.com to
HEAR chords, scales, and find more resources

220

G Dorian

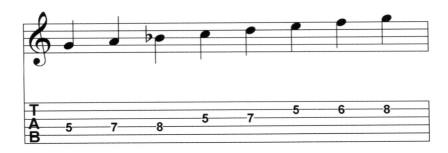

Scale pattern	G A B♭ C D E F G
	G F E D C B♭ A G

FREE ACCESS on smartphones, iPhone, Android etc.
Use any QR code app to scan this QR code

Or go straight to www.flametreemusic.com to
HEAR chords, scales, and find more resources

221

A
A#/B♭
B
C
C#/D♭
D
D#/E♭
E
F
F#/G♭
G
G#/A♭

G Minor Pentatonic

Scale pattern	G B♭ C D F G
	G F D C B♭ G

G Blues

Scale pattern	G B♭ C D♭ D♮ F G
	G F D♮ D♭ C B♭ G

A
A♯/B♭
B
C
C♯/D♭
D
D♯/E♭
E
F
F♯/G♭
G
G♯/A♭

G Phrygian

Scale pattern

G A♭ B♭ C D E♭ F G
G F E♭ D C B♭ A♭ G

G Locrian

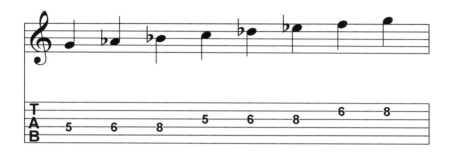

| Scale pattern | G A♭ B♭ C D♭ E♭ F G |
| | G F E♭ D♭ C B♭ A♭ G |

A
A♯/B♭
B
C
C♯/D♭
D
D♯/E♭
E
F
F♯/G♭
G
G♯/A♭

G Mixolydian

Scale pattern	G A B C D E F G
	G F E D C B A G

G Phrygian Major
(Spanish Gypsy)

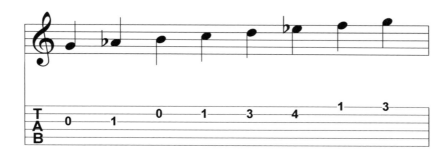

Scale pattern

G A♭ B C D E♭ F G
G F E♭ D C B A♭ G

Or go straight to www.flametreemusic.com to
HEAR chords, scales, and find more resources

A
A♯/B♭
B
C
C♯/D♭
D
D♯/E♭
E
F
F♯/G♭
G
G♯/A♭

G Lydian Dominant

Scale pattern	G A B C# D E F G
	G F E D C# B A G

FREE ACCESS on smartphones, iPhone, Android etc.
Use any QR code app to scan this QR code

Or go straight to www.flametreemusic.com to
HEAR chords, scales, and find more resources

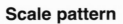

G Diminished

Scale pattern

G A♭ B♭ B♮ C♯ D E F G
G F E D C♯ B♮ B♭ A♭ G

A
A♯/B♭
B
C
C♯/D♭
D
D♯/E♭
E
F
F♯/G♭
G
G♯/A♭

G Chromatic

Scale pattern	G A♭ A♮ B♭ B♮ C C♯ D E♭ E♮ F F♯ G
	G F♯ F♮ E B♭ D C♯ C♮ B B♭ A A♭ G

FREE ACCESS on smartphones, iPhone, Android etc.
Use any QR code app to scan this QR code

230

Or go straight to www.flametreemusic.com to
HEAR chords, scales, and find more resources

G Wholetone

Scale pattern	G A B C# D# F G
	G F D# C# B A G

FREE ACCESS on smartphones, iPhone, Android etc.
Use any QR code app to scan this QR code

Or go straight to www.flametreemusic.com to
HEAR chords, scales, and find more resources

A

A#/Bb

B

C

C#/Db

D

D#/Eb

E

F

F#/Gb

G

G#/Ab

SCALES & MODES

G♯
A♭

A

A♯/B♭

B

C

C♯/D♭

D

D♯/E♭

E

F

F♯/G♭

G

G♯/A♭

FREE ACCESS on smartphones, iPhone, Android etc. Use any QR code app to scan this QR code

Or go straight to www.flametreemusic.com to **HEAR** chords, scales, and find more resources

A♭ Major

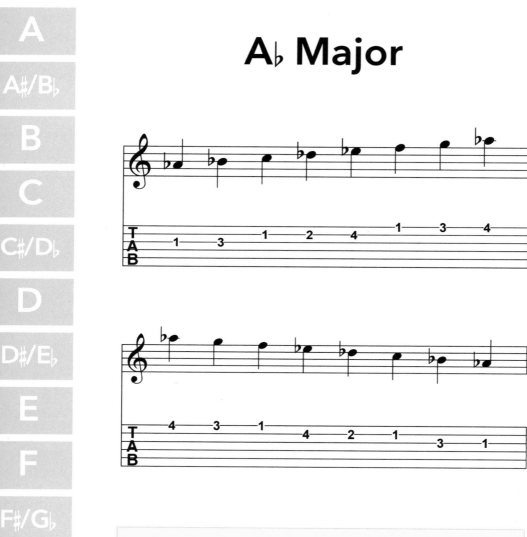

Scale pattern	A♭ B♭ C D♭ E♭ F G A♭
	A♭ G F E♭ D♭ C B♭ A♭

Or go straight to www.flametreemusic.com to **HEAR** chords, scales, and find more resources

A♭ Major Pentatonic

Scale pattern	A♭ B♭ C E♭ F A♭
	A♭ F E♭ C B♭ A♭

FREE ACCESS on smartphones, iPhone, Android etc.
Use any QR code app to scan this QR code

Or go straight to www.flametreemusic.com to
HEAR chords, scales, and find more resources

A♭ Lydian

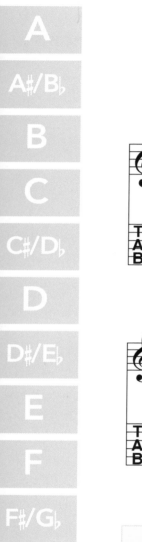

Scale pattern

A♭ B♭ C D E♭ F G A♭
A♭ G F E♭ D C B♭ A♭

FREE ACCESS on smartphones, iPhone, Android etc.
Use any QR code app to scan this QR code

Or go straight to www.flametreemusic.com to
HEAR chords, scales, and find more resources

A♭ Lydian Augmented

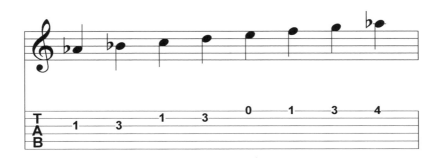

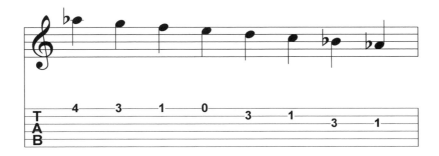

| **Scale pattern** | A♭ B♭ C D E F G A♭ |
| | A♭ G F E D C B♭ A♭ |

A

A♯/B♭

B

C

C♯/D♭

D

D♯/E♭

E

F

F♯/G♭

G

G♯/A♭

G♯ Natural Minor

| **Scale pattern** | G♯ A♯ B C♯ D♯ E F♯ G♯ |
| | G♯ F♯ E D♯ C♯ B A♯ G♯ |

Or go straight to www.flametreemusic.com to
HEAR chords, scales, and find more resources

G♯ Harmonic Minor

Scale pattern	G♯ A♯ B C♯ D♯ E F✕ G♯
	G♯ F✕ E D♯ C♯ B A♯ G♯

Or go straight to www.flametreemusic.com to
HEAR chords, scales, and find more resources

A

A♯/B♭

B

C

C♯/D♭

D

D♯/E♭

E

F

F♯/G♭

G

G♯/A♭

G# Melodic Minor

Scale pattern	G# A# B C# D# E# F× G#
	G# F# E♮ D# C# B A# G#

Or go straight to www.flametreemusic.com to **HEAR** chords, scales, and find more resources

G♯ Dorian

| **Scale pattern** | G♯ A♯ B C♯ D♯ E♯ F♯ G♯ |
| | G♯ F♯ E♯ D♯ C♯ B A♯ G♯ |

Or go straight to www.flametreemusic.com to
HEAR chords, scales, and find more resources

A

A♯/B♭

B

C

C♯/D♭

D

D♯/E♭

E

F

F♯/G♭

G

G♯/A♭

G♯ Minor Pentatonic

| **Scale pattern** | G♯ B C♯ D♯ F♯ G♯ |
| | G♯ F♯ D♯ C♯ B G♯ |

FREE ACCESS on smartphones, iPhone, Android etc.
Use any QR code app to scan this QR code

Or go straight to www.flametreemusic.com to
HEAR chords, scales, and find more resources

G♯ Blues

Scale pattern	G♯ B C♯ D♮ D♯ F♯ G♯
	G♯ F♯ D♯ D♮ C♯ B G♯

FREE ACCESS on smartphones, iPhone, Android etc.
Use any QR code app to scan this QR code

Or go straight to www.flametreemusic.com to
HEAR chords, scales, and find more resources

243

G♯ Phrygian

Scale pattern	G♯ A B C♯ D♯ E F♯ G♯
	G♯ F♯ E D♯ C♯ B A G♯

G♯ Locrian

| **Scale pattern** | G♯ A B C♯ D E F♯ G♯ |
| | G♯ F♯ E D C♯ B A G♯ |

A

A♯/B♭

B

C

C♯/D♭

D

D♯/E♭

E

F

F♯/G♭

G

G♯/A♭

A♭ Mixolydian

Scale pattern	A♭ B♭ C D♭ E♭ F G♭ A♭
	A♭ G♭ F E♭ D♭ C B♭ A♭

FREE ACCESS on smartphones, iPhone, Android etc.
Use any QR code app to scan this QR code

Or go straight to www.flametreemusic.com to
HEAR chords, scales, and find more resources

G♯ Phrygian Major
(Spanish Gypsy)

Scale pattern	G♯ A B♯ C♯ D♯ E F♯ G♯
	G♯ F♯ E D♯ C♯ B♯ A G♯

A
A♯/B♭
B
C
C♯/D♭
D
D♯/E♭
E
F
F♯/G♭
G
G♯/A♭

A♭ Lydian Dominant

Scale pattern	A♭ B♭ C D E♭ F G♭ A♭
	A♭ G♭ F E♭ D C B♭ A♭

FREE ACCESS on smartphones, iPhone, Android etc.
Use any QR code app to scan this QR code

Or go straight to www.flametreemusic.com to
HEAR chords, scales, and find more resources

A
A#/B♭
B
C
C#/D♭
D
D#/E♭
E
F
F#/G♭
G
G#/A♭

G♯ Diminished

| Scale pattern | G♯ A B C D D♯ E♯ F♯ G♯ |
| | G♯ F♯ E♯ D♯ D♮ C B A G♯ |

FREE ACCESS on smartphones, iPhone, Android etc.
Use any QR code app to scan this QR code

Or go straight to www.flametreemusic.com to
HEAR chords, scales, and find more resources

A

A♯/B♭

B

C

C♯/D♭

D

D♯/E♭

E

F

F♯/G♭

G

G♯/A♭

G♯ Chromatic

Scale pattern

G♯ A A♯ B B♯ C♯ C× D♯ E E♯ F♯ F× G♯
G♯ F× F♯ E♯ E♮ D♯ C× C♯ B♯ B♮ A♯ A♮ G♯

FREE ACCESS on smartphones, iPhone, Android etc.
Use any QR code app to scan this QR code

Or go straight to www.flametreemusic.com to
HEAR chords, scales, and find more resources

250

A♭ Wholetone

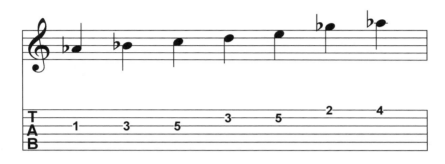

| **Scale pattern** | A♭ B♭ C D E G♭ A♭ |
| | A♭ G♭ E D C B♭ A♭ |

THE NEXT STEP

GOING ONLINE

Finally, you can go to www.flametreemusic.com
where you can find and listen to scales,
chords and other resources to help
you learn more as a musician.

A

A#/B♭

B

C

C#/D♭

D

D#/E♭

E

F

F#/G♭

G

G#/A♭

A

A#/B♭

B

C

C#/D♭

D

D#/E♭

E

F

F#/G♭

G

G#/A♭

FlameTreeMusic.com gives you a number of resources to complement this book:

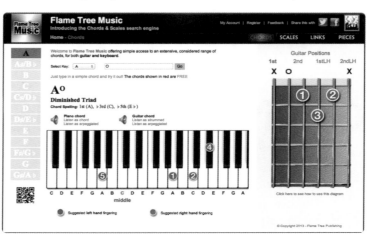

- A wide range of chords which can be **heard** in piano and guitar sounds.
- 20 core scales are provided for each key, again you can **hear** the notes played on the guitar and the piano.

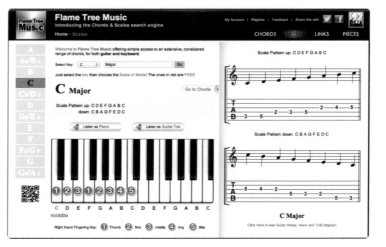

FREE ACCESS on smartphones, iPhone, Android etc. Use any QR code app to scan this QR code

Or go straight to www.flametreemusic.com to **HEAR** chords, scales, and find more resources

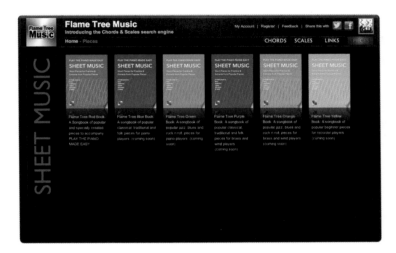

- **The Flame Tree Red book** offers over 100 pages of popular tunes and examples for the piano. It can be viewed online using a desktop computer, on a tablet such as an iPad, or on a smartphone such as an iPhone. Other books offer different selections of pieces for the piano and a variety of wind instruments.

- Other resources on the site include **links** and **book recommendations** to extend your knowledge. There are a great many excellent publications available, both in print and increasingly online. We'll update this resource frequently.

We're always looking for ways to improve what we do so please give us feedback on our Facebook page. www.facebook.com/flametreemusic.

FREE ACCESS on smartphones, iPhone, Android etc. Use any QR code app to scan this QR code

Or go straight to www.flametreemusic.com to **HEAR** chords, scales, and find more resources

255